Can Students End School Violence?
Solutions from America's Youth

The federal government _____ with the leading educational organizations, found _____ in _____ safe schools:

1. Most children who become violent towards themselves or others feel rejected and psychologically victimized.
2. Keeping children safe is a community wide effort.
3. Effective schools create environments where children and young people truly feel connected. Our common goal must be to reconnect with every child.

Letter to Principal and Teachers (August 22, 1998)
Thurston High School Springfield, OR
Early Warning: Timely Response-A Guide to Safe Schools

> RICHARD W. RILEY,
> Secretary of Education,
> United States Department of Education
>
> JANET RENO,
> Attorney General,
> United States Department of Justice

Most children who become violent towards self or others feel rejected and psychologically victimized. Tragic episodes of school violence are rare and an extreme outcome. But, subtle acts of violence-those that can lead to tragic events-are epidemic. This book presents ideas and actions to help all of us become better at being who we already are-powerful people who can influence our school communities, take responsibility for our actions, and create a safer future. Every action we take affects the greater community. The most significant social advances of our nation, founded on the belief that all men are created equal, shattered our inequalities and rocked the social structure of our great nation. It is time to move forward again, not because I say so, not because any one person says so, but because our generation can no longer tolerate social climates where any individual or group is made to suffer. Now is the time for us to connect, to come together as a self organizing group, to value the contribution that each and every person on this earth can make. When people are valued, they will contribute, they will make a difference. All schools have the potential to get better at creating connection and community-what it takes to prevent and end school violence. It starts with each one of us.

JASON R. DORSEY, Author, Can Students End School Violence?,
Founder, YouthConnect

What others are saying...

"Jason Dorsey has a remarkable life story to tell. He serves as a true inspiration to all ages, but especially to our youth."
-TOM GALLAGER, Commissioner of Ecucation, State of Florida

"Can Students End School Violence? provides the solutions from America's youth that communities have been waiting for! Jason knows how to connect with and inspire youth!"
-TONY CAMPBELL, Executive Director, Community Mobilization
America's Promise: The Alliance for Youth

"Jason Dorsey has made a difference in the values and perceptions of teachers and administrators alike. They and the students of West Virginia will be challenged to establish and achieve ever higher goals as a result."
-HENRY MAROCKIE, State Superintendent of Schools,
West Virginia Department of Education

"Jason is an extremely bright and energetic young man who makes a connection with youth. His enthusiasm and passion... is contagious. Jason Dorsey is a walking endorsement for his belief that every person has limitless potential and passion waiting to be unleashed."
-JOY GREENWOOD, Counselor, Gering Junior High, Nebraska

"Jason's book and live presentation are excellently planned and delivered with enough humor to make even the most exhausted participant feel relaxed and invigorated."
-JAMES M. WALKER, Director, National Resource Center for Youth Services
The University of Oklahoma

"What a hit! ...You reach students at their level, with the issues that impact them!"
-JEANNE T. WELLS, Vice President, ABI Foundation,
University of Business Horizons, Des Moines, Iowa

"Jason inspired and motivated. It's not hard to understand why he has such a large mentor support system made up of adults and youth alike."
-JOHN LUCAS, Director of Programs, Texas Education Agency

Golden Ladder ™ Productions

Archstone ™
Press

Archstone Press
Post Office Box 210752
Nashville, Tennessee 37221-0752

First Archstone Press/Golden Ladder™ Productions Co-Edition,
2000

Archstone Press is a registered trademark of
JayMar Services, LLC.

Designed by JayMar Services, LLC
Edited by Elota Patton, Greta Gardner
Cover Design by: Flaming Head Media, Austin TX

Printed in Colombia, South America
Panamericana Formas e Impresos S.A.

Library of Congress Catalog Number: 99-069683

Dorsey, Jason R.
        Can Students End School Violence?
        -Solutions from America's Youth

ISBN:1-929749-00-7

Can Students end school Violence?

Solutions From America's Youth

JASON R. DORSEY

Archstone Press™

Golden Ladder™
Productions

 For additional information, please visit:
endschoolviolence.com

"You taught us to remember why we became teachers-to make a difference in the lives of our youth! You have made a difference in our lives."
-Dr. Richard Irizarry, Assistant Superintendent,
Rio Grande City ISD, Texas

"I am inspired by your dedication to the youth of this country. You demonstrate by example your commitment to ensuring a healthy future for all of America's youth. You have wisdom well beyond your years."
-Kathleen Peters, Pinellas America's Promise:
The Alliance for Youth, St. Petersburg, Florida

"Your words are always fresh and to the point. ...thank you for your support of Boys Ranch and for ...your most important message."
-Mel Jones, Cal Farley's Boys Ranch

"Together we can build a brighter future for Austin and our youth."
-Kirk Watson, Mayor, City of Austin, Texas

"Your attitude and enthusiasm for school, work and life are characteristics we encourage our students to embrace. We look forward to using your book in classroom instruction and visiting your website on our student laptop computers."
-Terry Randolph, Superintendent of Education, Hancock County District, Klin, Missouri

"Your words were inspiring..."
-Lonnie R. Williams, Assistant Vice Chancellor for Student Services; Director, Youth Opportunities Unlimited, University of Arkansas

"The mere fact that this young, gifted and intelligent person makes so much sense and understands educational issues is astonishing. His age and mature attitude give him a distinct advantage in that his observations and views are so realistic. His great understanding and feelings for education and students make him a great asset to the educational profession. You use what he teaches."
-Carlos Lopez, Superintendent
Freer Independent School District, Texas

Dedication:

This book is dedicated to every person whose life has been impacted by school violence. Together we can connect and end the hurt,

Also...........

To my brother Randy and sister Alanna,
thank you for always believing in me.

To my Dad for caring about my future.

To my Mom, John, and Grandpa for always loving me.

To my mentors for their belief, guidance,
and unwavering support.
I will share your wisdom.

Acknowledgments:

This book was an entirely team based project. From the thousands of students who provided me with their insights, to my office staff, to the publishing team, and our non-profit organization, so many people helped to create the book and forthcoming initiative to end school violence. Thank you to everyone who worked so diligently to bring this project to fruition.

Special thanks to Sondra Ulin, my amazing marketing director, for her countless hours of work and talent in working with people. To the incredible editing team of Elota Patton and Greta Gardner, thank you for building this book. To Sharenda Roam for her creative input and expertise. To Gary Selvy and the support of The World Institute to End School Violence, we value your leadership. To our newest team member, Laura Traylor, for her belief and new perspective. To Jennifer Hill, for making public relations work. To our phenomenal publishing team leader, Jay Heinlein.

My incredible team of mentors that consistently help me to help others gave tremendous input to this project. They include Admiral Bobby Inman, Mark Meussner, Gary Selvy, Robert Floyd, Brad Armstrong, Elliott Beck, Jim Henry, Jerry Harris, Mike Sheridan, Dan Akers, Fred and Diane Akers, Tom Donini, Mike Connoway, Dr. Ratna Solomon, David Pruitt, Dr. Larry Faulkner, Jerry Stanley, Jill George, Bert Pluymen, Luther Parker, Herb Miller, Jerry Martin, Mark Victor Hansen, Jack Canfield, and Bob Hickerson.

The following people deserve much gratitude for their support: Ron Meyer, Arnold Williams, Art Merino, Pat Schwallie-Giddis, Angelos Angelou, Joseph Dial, Walt Tashnick, Fabrizio, Linda Rudwick, Teresa Esparza, and Mike Crixell.

To my good friends: Michael Tashnick, Robert Sek, Jimmy Ardoin, Joe Machemehl, Joshua Solomon, Sarah Dunn, Samantha Cooley, Shannon and Trey Owen, Jason Carter, Shannon Pickard, Kelly Anderson and Brandon Oliver.

Most importantly, to the many people who are working to end school violence. Thank you from the youth of America.

A Few Words for Parents and Educators:
How to Use This Book

School violence is a serious topic to every parent and educator in America. The latest incidents around the country have made all of us realize that this is not an isolated phenomenon. It doesn't only happen somewhere else. It starts small, even silently, and can build up. The potential for school violence is real, and we must work together to end it now.

Speaking in schools all across America, I see people working together to safeguard their children and their schools. New rules have mushroomed, regulating everything from clothes and backpacks to violence hotlines and metal detectors. All of these efforts are important. There is little that any parent or educator would not do to prevent tragedy in their school.

This book takes a different approach. Using systems thinking, the idea we're all connected, it looks at how each person in a group affects the group as a whole, and what each person in a group—or a school or a community—can do to stop school violence. This book helps students do something essential to ending school violence; it helps them learn to think about themselves as a part of a school culture and take responsibility for creating that culture; a culture of connection.

The book includes a series of thinking/teaching exercises that asks students to see their world, understand it, and influence it when necessary. It begins with systems thinking (the *Team Players* section), moves to communication and negotiation skills (*Straight Talkers* and *Peace Keepers*), and concludes with both adult and peer mentoring programs and life skills (*Life Winners*).

Can Student's End School Violence?, will help young people understand each other and the world we live in, then work together to change what's not useful. At the heart of this change is transforming the way we communicate with and think about one another.

The World Institute to End School Violence encourages students, parents, educators, and the community to jointly explore how we can harness a new kind of power, the power to change our world for the better. The greatest power we have.

This book will cover major issues related to ending school violence, like:

- Seeing the influence of social groups on school violence
- Building relationships among groups in the school system and beyond that can change the world
- Understanding the uses and abuses of emotions, how they can control us or we can manage them
- Raising students' self esteem through changes in behavior
- Teaching communication skills to help all people in our schools to be clear, straightforward, and considerate
- Using negotiation skills to improve school safety
- Finding mentors to explore interests and skills for personal growth
- Becoming mentors to share new ways to relate
- Creating a community where school violence is not acceptable to any member of the community
- Maintaining this new approach to school safety

Parent and Educator edition coming soon!

Four Cornerstones of Ending School Violence			
Team Players:	**Straight Talkers:**	**Peace Keepers:**	**Life Winners:**
Connect	*Communicate*	*Lead*	*Believe*
Systems Thinking	Open Communication	Negotiation in Action	Success and Empowerment

Working with so many youth and adults, I've realized that each group has its own style of communicating.

This book covers ideas essential for students and adults, but is written in a more personal style for youth. Every school system has its own advantages and limitations. Each person, classroom, and family is unique. To end school violence, students need to learn who they are and discover the resources they have and the ones they can create. Many of the readings, actions, and discussions in this book provide personal insight about the way young people view the world, and how they can learn from those insights to change their world.

There is no one cookie-cutter recipe or perfect book for ending school violence. Each school and community must draw on its unique resources to create a workable plan. The teachings in this book can bring people together to think about school violence. The action items will help each person and group build their own tailored plans for their school's survival, growth, and transformation.

Using this book, we can create a more connected, conscious, and caring society, a society that will end school violence.

Every Choice you make can affect your school community. You have in your hands, in your mind, and in your heart the power to create a more connected school community, and that's what it will take to end school violence.

Some Words for Us Young People

Every Choice you make can affect your school community. You have in your hands, in your mind, and in your heart the power to create a more connected school community, and that's what it will take to end school violence.

The last two years, I have traveled across this country speaking with young people about working to find career and life success. I have been to small schools and big ones, to cities and to rural areas, to the North and the South and to both coasts. As different as the people I've met are, we all share similar goals, fears and dreams. I, too, am a young person like you.

And everywhere I have visited, I've met young people who are eager and willing to help themselves and others. I've been excited, inspired, amazed and encouraged. The greatest thing I have learned in all my visits is that the young people of America are awesome. We're innovative, smart, persistent, and ready to do what it takes to make the world a better place for our friends, our schools, our communities, and ourselves.

As most of you know, during the past couple of years there have been some emotional episodes of violence in schools. We've all seen it on TV. Many of us have talked it over with our friends and families. Our schools have taken action to protect us from this threat of school violence.

Young people from all over the country have told me that they are concerned, that they want to stop school violence. Many of them have come up with great ideas. This book is the result of all of the listening and discussion that I have done with young people around America. *It is our answer to ending school violence.* We have the power to take responsibility and create solutions. Working together, caring about one another, we can relate to each other in ways that will make all of us safer. But learning to relate in new ways means making changes.

I'm not saying that changing is the easiest thing in the world to do. We all have ideas or ways of acting that make us feel comfortable. Some of these will remain strong, while others may need to be improved. By working together with other young people and thinking through what we can do to change, we can learn to be

• Team Players:	Connect
• Straight Talkers:	Communicate
• Peace Keepers:	Lead
• Life Winners:	Believe

The key to ending school violence is to CONNECT with each other and share responsibility for creating the kind of school we want to attend. We can make the world a safer place for ourselves, our families, our friends and neighbors, and all the students who follow us. By working together, connecting and caring, we will end school violence.

Jason Ryan Dorsey

What's Inside

CORNERSTONE 2

– Straight Talkers: Walk the Talk

CORNERSTONE 3

– Peace Keepers: Stand Up For Each Other

CORNERSTONE 4

Life Winners: Prepare for the Future

Introduction

There they are... on the six o'clock news: frightened, confused faces of our youth, reflecting the unthinkable tragedy that has inexplicably unfolded before them. Educators, parents, community leaders, passers-by; all dazed, mystified, searching for answers. This scene, regrettably is being repeated again and again in rural America; in the inner- city; in "suburbia," what was seemingly a safe, peaceful suburban setting.

Violence amongst our youth plays out every day in America, and yes, across the globe. No, it doesn't always end in the catastrophic scenes reflected on television.

Violence may be reflected in things as subtle as name-calling, isolation or loss of hope. So, what is happening here? What can be done? I suspect that there is hardly anyone that hasn't been affected by violence in our schools **AND OUR COMMUNITIES**. Many great thinkers, academics, community leaders and public policy-makers have reviewed, researched, written and spoke on the cause and yes, even solutions to this issue. And yet, school violence continues.

Now we have a fresh, new view, from *the perspective of youth.* Jason Dorsey has reflected on and written on violence through their eyes, Using incredible youth input, Jason shares practical action oriented solutions to ending school violence.First, identifying in-depth issues and then building systemic, life-long solutions to resolving them.

The next edition of this book will include sections directly for educators, parents and community leaders. After surviving numerous life hurdles and personally feeling the tragedy of violence amongst his friends, Jason committed his life to helping others. After authoring his first book- *Graduate to Your Perfect Job*, he spent the next two years talking to and interacting with over 150,000 students all over America. What he saw and experienced was not total dismay, chaos and a general decline of our youth as is so often reported. To the contrary, *he witnessed great hope and desire to succeed.* Jason has carefully woven that hope and desire into this book. Ever mindful of the fragile line between success and failure in the daily lives of youth, he has crafted a message of positive solutions, support-structures, and parent, teacher and community involvement.

Jason's dream is to initially communicate his message through this book to every middle school and high school, both public and private throughout America.

Over a million copies of this book will be given free to

schools in the hope that these solutions will catch hold. This book is just the beginning. To create change takes involvement.

Jason so passionately believes in this important message that he is creating the ***Internet destination to deal with this issue*** **www.endschoolviolence.com.** ***This website will become the resource for students, parents, educators and communities. It will feature an interactive national database of ending school violence initiatives:***

- ***free downloadable copies of this book***
- ***bulletin boards for successful strategies***
- ***links to appropriate sites***
- ***scholarship contests based on volunteerism***
- ***news relative to this issue***
- ***advice from Jason and other experts***
- ***youth organizations membership information***
- ***and much more, fun, cool stuff!***

The non-profit - ***World Institute to End School Violence*** is helping to support these and other ongoing efforts.

Whether you are a student, educator, parent or community leader, I encourage you to read this book and invest yourself in making a positive difference.

We can all do something to end school violence. We need your help.

Gary M. Selvy, Chairman
World Institute to End School Violence

The Four Cornerstones for Youth

Team Players:	**Straight Talkers:**	**Peace Keepers:**	**Life Winners:**
Connect	*Communicate*	*Lead*	*Believe*
Systems Thinking	Open Communication	Negotiation in Action	Success and Empowerment

Four Cornerstones of Ending School Violence

Team Players:

Connect

Systems Thinking

CORNERSTONE 1

Team Players: We're All Connected

The Big Picture:
What is School Violence and
What Can I Do About It?

America's schools have a challenge: ending school violence. It's tough to talk about, and some people believe it can't change—it's not their problem. Some people even think, "Violence can't happen here. Nothing will ever go wrong with our students!"

But violence affects all of us, and there are steps we can take to end it. We've all seen on TV how violence can hurt people and those they care about. But school violence comes in all sizes. Negative comments, jealousy and blame, shoving and name-calling are also kinds of violence. We've all heard about people taking drugs or drinking to be cool. They even use it as an excuse to say, "It wasn't my fault!" if they hurt someone or cause an accident. Have you ever heard anyone make a comment about someone who didn't have the same skin color, clothes, or home life? Do any of your friends feel hurt or bad because another person has said something mean? Practically everybody has seen someone get hit or punched.

"We are the solution. By getting connected, we can end school violence."

Some kids even want to hurt themselves. All of these are examples of school violence. Ignoring smaller bits of violence in school allows violence to build up. Then that melting pot of mean acts and hurt feelings might become a situation waiting to explode. It's up to us to prevent problems from piling up by acting now to end school violence. Recently, I talked to a young man who had attended a school where violence occurred. He remembered the boy who changed all of their lives as quiet, nicely dressed, and disconnected. I'll never forget what the survivor told me, "I think about him every day. I remember how quiet he was, and how alone.

I wish every day that I could go back in time and just speak to him, let him know that I cared. I really believe it would have made a difference." Violence is the problem. We are the solution. By getting connected, we can end school violence.

Action:

1. Is there anyone in your school who usually gets overlooked?
2. Could you take time to say "hello" to them?
3. What would it take for you to say "hello" to them?

The Four Cornerstones:
Overcoming Violence and Winning in Life

Ending school violence is a heroic idea, but some people want to know, "What's in it for me?" Some of us may be thinking right now, "Hey, it's not my problem," or, "I'm only one person. How can I make a difference?" or, "I'm just not interested."

Well, the bonus is that the Four Cornerstones to end violence are also the building blocks we all need to become winners in the game of life.

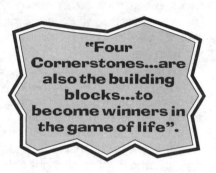

"Four Cornerstones...are also the building blocks...to become winners in the game of life".

Everyone knows the saying; "The children are our future." Well, we were those children, we are the students, and we soon will be the future of this country. To get where we want to go in the future, we need the mind set and skills of the Four Cornerstones. We need to become Team Players, Straight Talkers, Peace Keepers and Life Winners.

How do the Four Cornerstones work?

—Team Players

First of all, it's important learn to connect with other people, to become Team Players. Team players gain by relying on the support of others and supporting them. There is a saying, "One twig alone can be broken. A bundle of twigs is unbreakable." In any team, strength comes in many forms, but it's always about using the skills and talents of different people for the good of the whole group. Team players help their friends move furniture, solve math problems, campaign in school elections, repair bikes, and more.

The best team players know that helping people learn to solve their own problems makes life easier for everybody. Teams can be small student groups, a family, neighborhood or other organizations, or the school as a whole. Teams can be many groups working together for the same goal, like teachers, students and parents working on a prom. ***Team players succeed because they join together with others to achieve a goal.*** Creating real teams means that everybody wins.

—Straight Talkers

Second, it's important to get our own ideas and feelings across to other people, to become Straight Talkers. ***Straight Talkers*** can make a point without hurting others. They have the communication skills to think before they act. They understand the feelings that often fuel arguments and have the skills to disarm verbal conflict. Combining caring for others with the skills to talk through tough situations can help us manage our world in new ways.

Straight talkers put new behaviors in place of old ones, respond in new, constructive ways to gossip, criticism, and verbal attack. Straight talkers use words and gestures to help other people understand their views: they want to be clear. They think hard about ***what*** to say, ***how*** to say it, ***who*** to say it to, and ***why*** they need to make that point in the first place.

In other words, straight talkers are the people we want for friends, parents, teachers and mentors. They know who they are and what they feel, and they care about what other people feel, too. They are great communicators who treat themselves and other people with respect.

—Peace Keepers

Third, to end violence, we must practice becoming ***Peace Keepers.*** We might think, "Hey, this isn't my fault!" It's easy to blame violence on other people and then wait for some expert to fix things, but it won't work. We can't ignore reality or expect a magical solution. Only we can stop violence from happening, through straight talk and team playing. Peace Keepers are powerful allies. They feel good about themselves with friends, teachers, and parents—actually, with ***everybody,*** in their own groups or outside of them.

Being a Peace Keeper means standing up for what we believe and for what others believe. It means backing up what we say by acting on our beliefs. This may mean walking away from a bad situation to stay safe, or helping a friend through tough times. "Walking our talk" helps us lead by example, which is really powerful. When we stand up for safe schools, it helps others to stand up, too. To end school violence, **Peace Keepers** never use violence. We use communication skills to make friendships, to learn together, and to enjoy life. We use negotiation skills to help manage confrontation, anger, and fear, our own and others'.

Peace Keepers don't let mean words and acts separate different groups. We create a place where different people can listen to each other and learn, where first and foremost, people care about each other.

—Life Winners

Finally, we all want to stand out and use our own special talents to build happy lives. Few people strive to be average. Everyone deserves to live their dream. We all want to be **Life Winners.** You know what? We can.

Life Winners have a goal of living meaningful lives, being happy, and helping others. Each of us is unique, the only one of us ever on the planet. Our minds grow and change each day. We have so many skills; we probably don't even know yet what some of them can produce. By exploring different paths, we can take advantage of the world around us. When we jump into learning about what we might like to do, we'll find out what we can do. And if we connect with other people at the same time, we can become unstoppable.

Some people may be thinking, "Me? What can I do?" That's where mentors can help. Mentors are the experts and coaches in the skills you want to explore. They are people who sincerely believe in young people and share what they know to help people learn and achieve.

Using our own special abilities, we can be mentors, too. In fact, we've probably already helped someone else learn something. That's being a mentor. We just may not have thought about ourselves that way. People who help others learn about what they can do are truly life winners.

We can use the **Four Cornerstones to help each other** and to help end school violence. By working on each cornerstone, we can build strong foundations for our lives. When we all work together on those foundations, the sky is no longer the limit.

Action:

1. Who do you know that is a team player?
2. Who do you know that is a good listener?
3. Who do you know that can resolve arguments?
4. Do you feel prepared to succeed in your future?

Idea 3:

Perspective:
We All See The Same World Differently

We're all unique, no matter how much we sometimes seem the same. We've had different families growing up, our dreams about the future all have our own personal touch, our backgrounds are unique, and our beliefs are individual. Our experiences have helped us understand and get ahead at home, in school or with friends. Based upon all our life experiences, we create standards to make our own choices and to live by. These standards become our "personal disciplines" and they help us decide right from wrong, guide our life, and lead our interactions with other people.

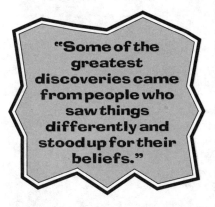

"Some of the greatest discoveries came from people who saw things differently and stood up for their beliefs."

Personal disciplines help us set up a strategy or plan for new situations, and provide us with a way to learn about new people or things. Personal disciplines are the best rules we know for living. That's the good part. The bad news is that some personal disciplines stop us from exploring new things.

Once we have a certain idea or opinion, it is sometimes tough to understand why others don't see things our way. But, if everyone thought and acted the same way, the world would be pretty boring. How could we ever learn from anyone else if everyone thought the same? There would be no new ideas! Some of the greatest discoveries came from people who saw things differently and stood up for their beliefs!

To get support for our ideas, we need to talk in a way that other people understand. Everybody grasps new ideas from their own point of view or mental model. The secret to getting our ideas across is to put it into words and ideas that other people understand. So how do we find out the way somebody else understands things? We listen to them. We learn about the ideas and feelings other people have about the same idea or problem. The more we try to understand what other people are thinking, the more respect they will show us, and the better they'll listen to our ideas. We do not all have to agree. We just need to understand and respect that everyone can see the same thing, yet see it uniquely and differently. The more we try to understand other people's views, the stronger we can connect with them.

##

1. Think about one idea you have that not everyone agrees with.
2. How do you deal with the people who do not agree with your idea?
3. Have you ever taken time to listen to their ideas?

Acceptance:
The Last One Picked

Imagine going to a new school for the first time. How do you deal with the new teachers, new classes, and other students? Many of us get stressed about what other people might think of us, what we wear or how we talk. What will the other students be like? Will we make new friends we can trust?

Meeting new people and figuring out where we fit in can be frustrating and stressful. Without even knowing us, some people may judge us because of one little thing, like if we're shy or tall. We all know somebody who has been accepted immediately, who can meet people and get into any group he or she wants. But for most of us, it takes an awkward time of being "the new kid" before we finally make friends.

"We're all different, but we all need to be included and valued"

Imagine going to the same school for many years and *never* being completely accepted, maybe feeling constantly alone. Loneliness affects our feelings about ourselves, our grades, even about our family. One cause of school violence is people feeling out of place and not accepted.

Many of us wear styles that are different, or like different kinds of music. A few of us spend all our time with close friends and nobody else.

We all grow up. But good friends, friends that we've had for a long time, are often "true friends." A true friend shares feelings and adventures. A true friend will still be our friend even if we have a fight. *A true friend is someone we can trust.* We might grow in different directions, maybe not even hang with the same group anymore, but if we ever really need those true friends, they'll be there. *Knowing that there's someone, who accepts us no matter what, really helps us move forward in school and life.*

To have a true friend, we also have to be one. That means staying a friend even when we move in different directions.

Accepting people for who they are and where they are

in life gives both them and us a chance to open up and trust each other. We're all different, but we all need to be included and valued. If we all made time to accept other students, people would feel less alone and our schools would be safer.

Action:

1. Do you have a true friend? How did you meet them?
2. How long did it take for you to trust them?
3. Is there anyone at your school who might need a friend like you? Someone they could trust.

Idea 5:

Groups:
We All Want to Belong

Groups have a big impact on how we act around other people. Because all people have a strong need to belong, we feel more secure with our friends. When we're with them, we feel good about ourselves. On the other hand, sometimes we judge people. If they can't do the things we do, if they talk or act differently, if they don't have the right sneakers, they're weird; they don't belong.

Groups, since they're made up of a bunch of us, include more kinds of skills and abilities than any one of us alone. This gives a group more strength than a single person and a different style than other groups. Powerful groups—those with lots of members or special skills, things, or abilities—can pick and choose their members. As groups get stronger, they can offer more sense of identity, or more protection.

"Wanting to belong to a group is a natural part of growing up, learning to be with others, exploring who we are."

That's why we may want to join a group; it's also why it may be hard to get in.

There is an important reason why groups protect their differences, and it has everything to do with ending school violence. People tend to come together and build trust based upon what they agree on-similarities. They also tend to separate around differences-what they disagree on. This can create a problem. It can cause us to reject people who can help us learn new things and sometimes forces us to live by stereotypes.

Powerful groups want to keep their power, so group members show off their differences from other groups, and let us into the group—or not—based on whether we fit in. Being accepted by a group helps us feel like we belong. Groups create their own rules—spoken and unspoken—for things like how to dress, talk, gesture, relate to the opposite sex, relate to parents or to other groups.

Groups, whether big or small, use skills, style, looks and more as a source of power. Violence—acting in ways that hurt or intimidate or frighten others—*is a big source of power.* It's also an abuse of power. Many groups feel that to get what they want, they must use put-downs, intimidation, or bullying. They may use it to keep their territory, like a hangout or a certain part of the cafeteria.

Wanting to belong to a group is a natural part of growing up, learning to be with others, and exploring who we are. As we grow, and adults trust us to be away from home more (or we're in situations where we have to be alone), friends become more and more important. Knowing who we like helps us know who we are. And learning who we are is one of the big tasks of teens.

But groups can be dead ends, too. A group may not be bad, but always having to be the same as everyone else may not let us explore and grow. The people we surround ourselves with reveal a great deal about us. To end school violence, we must be open up to and appreciate people outside of our regular group.

Action:

1. Do you have a regular group of friends that you hang out with?
2. Does your regular group of friends exclude or make fun of other groups or people?
3. Have you ever stood up for the person or group that is being made fun of?

Idea 6:

Seeing The Good In People

Everyone has something good about them; even people we may not like.

Instead of trying to find that good in others, some people actually look for just the negative in other people. Some try, in our competitive society, to find other people's weakness so they can feel stronger or superior. Many times the way we look outside is used to judge our inside. How we dress, who we hang out with, and our looks can lead to judgments and stereotypes.

The key is to see people for who they are and not what they wear or who they hang around. ***The best leaders I know value people for their talents, not their weaknesses.***

It's easy to look at someone's appearance, fit him or her into some stereotype, and then go on with your life. But it's smarter and harder to take time to get to know someone, and realize his or her true goodness.

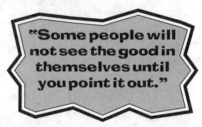

"**Some people will not see the good in themselves until you point it out.**"

Everyone I have ever met, regardless of his/her past actions or beliefs, has had something good to offer society. If nothing else, they were willing to share how they became so negative. Many of their suggestions are included in this book in an effort to keep other people from thinking and acting in ways that hurt people.

To end school violence we need to put our stereotypes and defenses aside to see the good in all people and truly value them. Seeing the good in other people is a key to building trust and working together to end school violence. We all have something good to offer.

Action:

1. Think of one good quality about yourself.
2. Think of one good quality about a friend of yours.
3. Think of one good quality about someone in your class that you normally don't talk to and ask yourself, "Could I tell them ?"

Idea 7:

We're All Connected,
Whether We Know It or Not

We are all riding on the same huge flying globe. Because of this, every part of our world actually has a relationship with every other part. If we cut down forests, people may get more trees to build houses, but a lot of animals lose their habitats. When a lot of cars get driven in a city, people can go places, but pollution builds up. When you change one part of a system, it affects the system as a whole.

Every one of us is part of many bigger systems. We all go to school, live in neighborhoods, have families of one kind or another, live in a state, live in the United States, live on planet earth. Looking more closely, we're all part of smaller parts within our own school system.

"Every part of our world actually has a relationship with every other part."

"We're all connected."

People tend to get together around shared interests, and when they do, groups form. Groups can form by design (the Drama Club decides to put on a play), or by accident (people discover they share interests and just start to hang out together).

Any change in a system can affect the whole group, but the change may or may not be for the good of the group. If you are a star in a team sport, you can play to look great but not support the team. If you play to make the whole team work together, you'll be a real star.

Every action we take affects other people in our school. This idea of being connected means that each of us can take actions that help to build a safer school for everyone.

Action:

Imagine a time when something you did changed a system in some way or when you saw someone else take an action that changed a system.

1. Can you think of something that happened at your school that affected your whole school?
2. Can you think of something you did that helped make your school safer for everyone?
3. What is something you could do soon to make your school safer for everyone?

Information:
The Breakfast of Champions

Every team has goals. Whether the team is just two people or more, we all want to survive and grow. In order to grow, we have to take stuff in: air, food, water, information, whatever. For instance, if someone wants to get better at math, that person would have to do their homework, pay attention in class, and learn the new material. We have to let new information come in if we want to grow.

"We have to let in new information in order for each of us to become the... very best we can be."

We also have to take in new energy and information to get our needs met. To do that, we have to notice what's happening right now, this very moment. If we get stuck trying to be who someone else thinks we should be, we may never be the person we truly are. If we don't learn, it's hard to react to new situations, whether the new situations are dangers or opportunities. We have to let in new information in order for each of us to make the most of opportunities. We are all given the chance to learn and help other people. Information is the key to both.

Action:

1. What is something you have learned that has helped you to help other people?
2. What kind of information do you think is most valuable to helping other people?
3. How do you normally get information?

Straight Talkers:

Communicate

Open Communication

CORNERSTONE 2

Straight Talkers: Walk the Talk

Idea 9:

Straight Talkers Listen as Well as Speak

To build safer schools, we need to know how to communicate in "straight talker" way. When we talk, we want other people to not just hear us; we want them to *listen*. **Straight Talkers** listen as well as speak, and stay focused on the discussion at hand. Straight talkers use their words and gestures to **connect with** other people and understand their views. This means thinking about what to say and how to say it. Although this doesn't mean agreeing with everything someone else says, it does mean taking the time to think about other people's ideas.

Straight Talkers speak their ideas in a non-threatening way. They're clear about what they want us to listen to and honest about how they feel. Straight talkers are definitely not hurtful or mean to other people. Before they speak, they think about their own and other people's

"When we talk, we want other people to not just hear us; we want them to listen."

feelings. **Rather than telling other people** how they should feel, straight talkers *ask* how they feel.

Straight talkers have talents they have learned and practiced—on purpose or not—to become effective speakers. They're fair, strong and understanding. They know what they think and how they feel. They consider other people's feelings. When we have problems, we get in touch with them. They care about how we feel. Many of us would like straight talkers to be our friends, parents, teachers and mentors. That's because straight talkers are great communicators. They listen to our ideas and respect us.

We can connect and feel comfortable with them. By becoming straight talkers ourselves, we help end school violence. It is only by **talking and listening** that we can understand other people's mindsets, lifestyles and goals. Friendships grow when we show someone that we care about how they feel and what they think.

Action:

1. How do you feel when someone that you care about doesn't listen to you?
2. Is there someone in your school who doesn't talk much?
3. Would you be willing to listen to them if they needed someone to talk with?

Changing Our Behavior:
"Get out of my way! I'm comfortable!"

Everyone says it: being a teenager is challenging. Our bodies are changing, we have things to do, and we get pressure from all sides to do them. We live in the world of the information superhighway, where change happens faster than anyone a generation ago could have imagined.

In many ways, all these changes are exciting. Many of us not only accept change we hunger for it. The teen years are a time when young people make test flights from the security of our family to test our abilities in a larger field. It's exciting. Lots of people say that these are the best years of our lives, but they can also be the toughest. Maybe they've forgotten how stressful, how difficult all this change and pressure can be.

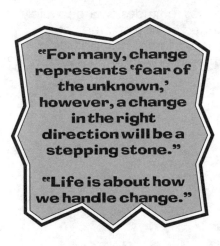

"For many, change represents 'fear of the unknown,' however, a change in the right direction will be a stepping stone."

"Life is about how we handle change."

We have to learn where we fit in, who our new friends will be. We have to choose all over again what activities we'll do, who to hang out with, what's cool and what's not. All of us want to find a comfort zone, a way of living-"a safe place" where we can safely continue to explore who we are becoming in the world.

We like these comfort zones. They help us to know who we are. They allow us to feel safe and avoid trouble. Comfort zones are great, but they have a downside. What if we're one of those people who can't find a comfort zone in the midst of all these changes? Or someone who never stretches his or her comfort zones?

The most common year to drop out of high school is the ninth grade. That's because ninth grade is a big year of change. In many schools, it's the transition year between grade school and high school. In a way, it's the first year we become young adults. It's a time when who we hang out with suddenly seems to take on more importance, and when we start identifying ourselves by the groups we belong to. But, what if we don't feel like we belong?

At this point, a few of us are probably asking, "What does all this talk about change have to do with school violence? I feel safe and have lots of friends." But let's talk about change. Change has **everything** to do with school violence. The people most likely to be tempted to do violence—of any kind—are the people who can't manage or deal with change. Our world, our friends, and ourselves are going to change as long as we live. To end school violence, we may have to change some of our actions and attitudes.

Action:

1. Have any of your friends' attitudes changed lately?
2. How have you changed in the last three years?
3. Find a picture of you from three years ago.
   Do you look or feel different now than three years ago?

Idea 11:

Media and Youth
—Read All About It!
(What Sells and What to Do About It)

We often hear people blaming movies, TV, music or the news for their endless stories on youth and violence. They say the media causes a lot of this violence. So how can students stop the trend? There are a lot of ideas, but two possible solutions are:

Change the channel or spend less time watching and listening to violence. The record companies, video game manufacturers and movie marketers all make money based on how many people buy or watch their product. Some people get so fascinated with violence they get hooked. In the case of a violent TV show, ratings go up as more people watch the show. The more people watch, the more producers can charge to run commercials. This brings in more money, and the cycle goes on.

"What Bleeds Leads."

The media wants people to pay attention. They have a responsibility to communicate information relevant to our society. Sure, the media may be "just" reporting events or giving people the shows or music they want, but if we weren't so fascinated by youth violence, it would not always be on the screen or in the headlines. The old expression, "What bleeds, leads!" still describes what sells in our society. If we lower the ratings for violent stories by not watching them, fewer will be featured.

End violence committed by youth. If youth do not commit violence, there will be no stories for the news media to report. *No violence by youth = no headlines about youth violence.* The news media isn't picking on youth because we are so bad, although it sometimes seems that way. Usually, they are just after higher ratings. They report events shaping our world, and right now we sell. Our society seems to be addicted to violence involving young people. Some stories the media offer us about violence in people our age are particularly disturbing.

Simply, If we want the news media and entertainment industry to stop focusing on youth violence, we need to stop youth from supporting entertainment that glorifies violence and youth need to quit committing acts of violence. Then the media will have to find another topic. Sounds simple, but it will take all of our efforts.

The entertainment industry has a responsibility to make money and the news media has a responsibility to report the news. We as consumers have a responsibility to influence "what" is purchased and reported and "how" youth are portrayed in the entertainment industry and the news media.

Action:

1. Have you ever seen youth violence in the media?
2. How did watching the violence make you feel?
3. Do you think that the movie, song, or news media fairly portrayed youth or reported the story; or did they "glamorize" the violence?

R-E-S-P-E-C-T:
What It Means To You And Me

It seems like "respect" is a word we've heard since the day we were born. We're told to respect our elders, respect other people, respect others' space, and respect our differences. Some of us, however, are not getting the message. When we gossip, act rude, make fun of people, or put down their friends or family, we're not respecting them. It's one thing to make jokes; it's entirely another when we make jokes at someone else's expense. Plus, the person making the joke usually looks worse or more insecure in the end. When we treat someone disrespectfully, we ignore what it takes to build strong people and communities.

Everyone, regardless of title, money, intelligence, whatever, should be treated with respect. *The most successful people I know respect people for being themselves.* They make everyone feel important, because in their minds, everyone

"**Respect...to earn it you must show it.**"
"**Everyone is important.**"

IS important. That is why people believe in them and have helped them become successful. We are all unique. By not respecting someone else, we deny attempts to build friendships, because we are basically saying, "I don't care about you." Sometimes we treat those closest to us with the least respect. It's those we care about the most who should be treated with the greatest respect. To end school violence, we must respect other people and realize that everyone is important.

Action:

1. How do people show respect at your school?
2. How do you feel when someone respects you?
3. Who is one person in your school that you respect?

Verbal and Non-Verbal Communication: "Stop Pointing Your Finger At Me!"

Everything about us – what we do, how we look, what we say – sends messages to other people. When we meet somebody for the first time, we "check them out." The kind of clothes we wear, the way our hair is cut, the music we like, the way we move, our favorite TV shows—these all send messages about who we are. Every moment we're alive, we see, hear, and get a sense of **who other people are** through all the information we take in from the world. And other people look at each of us and see the *me* each of us sends out into the world. On top of all that, we talk to each other. We whisper, shout and sing. We show our feelings in our voices: joy or sadness, fear or anger. Our bodies move to back up our opinions, to protect ourselves or to push into someone else's space. **So how we "act"** when we speak tells people that we mean what we say.

There are also times when "body language" tells us that someone doesn't mean what they speak, like when they say, "This game's really cool," with a bored look, or "I'm not mad!" while yelling at someone.

"Stop Pointing Your Finger At Me!" "Everything we do sends messages to other people."

When we talk with another person, we usually look at their face for clues to how they feel, like smiles or frowns. We watch how their hands "talk"—crossed at their chest to defend themselves, or open and willing to listen. People's voices can be high or low, sharp or smooth with different accents. All of this can give us a fairly good idea about how a person is feeling. Sometimes people's gestures tell you they want to be left alone even though they're not using words. Sometimes a person even says great things about you, but the message of their tone or movement can make you think that they don't mean what they say. Not meaning what you say weakens communication.

Straight talkers pay attention to what they say and **how they say it**, and they keep their word.

Action:

1. Say out loud, "I like peanut butter!" as if you <u>really</u> meant it.
2. Say out loud, "I like peanut butter..." as if you really don't care.
3. Say out loud, "I like peanut butter..." as if you <u>really don't</u> like it.

Gossip: "Psst - Did You Know That...?"

When people are together long enough to start trusting each other, they tend to share their feelings, observations, and ideas with each other; they don't hold back. Trust can grow in any setting: work, family, school, wherever. Open communication can lead to trust and learning, but some communication—gossip—is not open. It takes place in secret, behind closed doors, in whispers and snickers. This kind of communication can lead to rumors, revenge, or even violence.

Good news about people spreads at a natural rate among friends. Negative information rushes like the speed of light—nothing sells like the "inside scoop." In school, rumors can be especially bad. Did you ever go into a class and hear a group of people sharing the latest gossip?

"When people are together long enough to start trusting each other, they tend to share their feelings, observations, and ideas with each other."

Usually it's not even true! Gossip hurts and twists the truth. Few good things result from gossip.

Why do people gossip? Spreading rumors can sometimes briefly increase the gossip's popularity, because many people are curious to know more about other people. But saying mean things also makes people scared to be around the person saying them. When gossip is meant to put somebody down, we hurt people by repeating it.

Gossip hurts people. Many of us don't trust people who gossip or spread ugly rumors about other people. Even if the person who tells us the latest news is our friend, sometimes we wonder if they'll turn around and talk about us to someone else. Besides, it's hard to tell a friend like that about problems we might be having, since our problems might just become more gossip.Gossip breaks trust and friendships.

Action:

1. What is a rumor that you have heard recently?
2. Who told you?
3. Do you trust the person who told you the rumor "more" or "less" after spreading the rumor?

Read Minds? No Way!

Have you ever seen a "mind reader" on TV? Did you believe them- that they were for real? Sometimes we unintentionally imagine that we can read minds and assume that we know what someone is thinking by their tone of voice or the look on their face. **This can really cause problems.** In fact, if we imagine someone's having mean thoughts about us, we might even get mad about what we imagine. Or we might feel scared if we think someone wants to hurt us.

But what we feel in these situations is not about what the other person really thinks; it's about what we imagine they think. Some of us walk around feeling pretty stressed because of what we imagine other people are thinking. This is not straight-talking with ourselves. It's creating a fantasy in our heads and then acting as if the fantasy were true.

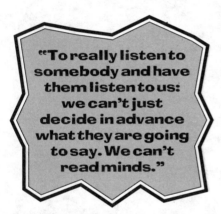

"To really listen to somebody and have them listen to us: we can't just decide in advance what they are going to say. We can't read minds."

So what do we do about this kind of mind reading? We can do one of two things. First, we can accept the fact that **we don't know what the other person thinks**, admit we just don't know. Although not knowing can cause some stress, it's not nearly as upsetting as feeling angry because we think someone doesn't like us. Second, we can ask the person if they are thinking what we are assuming they are thinking. This takes courage. It also has to be done carefully. We have to listen and ask questions, if we're not sure what someone means. If someone asks what we mean, or how we are feeling, we need to tell them the truth.

Action:

1. Have you ever assumed that someone was mad at you, when they really weren't.
2. Has anyone ever assumed something about you that was wrong?
3. How did you or how could you let them know the truth?

Idea 16:

Listening:
Everybody Wants to be Heard

Listening is the biggest part of talking. Seems funny, but it's true. It's frustrating when we tell something important to another person and they don't pay attention! How do we know they're not listening? Easy! Maybe they're looking around the room or rolling their eyes. Maybe you ask them a question and they say "Huh?" Now imagine if you had something super important to tell your best friend and your friend didn't want to listen. How frustrating!

We all need someone to listen. But not only listen: we need someone to care about what we have to say. In our speeding "information age," we've learned how to process a ton of news. That's because there's so much of it! TV, radio, CD's, newspapers, magazines, the Internet—new information comes at us continually. We've also learned how to block information out. To survive this information overload, we numb ourselves to it, cut ourselves off. But, there's a side effect to this numbing down; we may lose contact with live people.

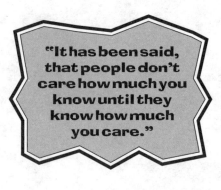

"It has been said, that people don't care how much you know until they know how much you care."

The basis of any friendship or team effort is trust. ***Building trust means actively listening to and respecting the thoughts and feelings of others***. To show respect when listening, we focus on what another person is saying, clear away distractions, make eye contact, nod and lean forward and use other cues that let them know we hear them. A true sign of leadership is not how well we speak, but how well we listen.

Think about who your best friends are, or the people you would call first if you had terrific news. They are probably the ones who listen to you and care about you—without hidden agendas. Sincere listening is essential to ending school violence. Listening helps us to focus on someone beside ourselves, builds trust, and shows that we value the other person. We may not always agree, but we can always learn. The best talkers are the people who listen.

Action:

1. How do you let someone know that you are listening to them?
2. Do you ever not listen when someone is talking to you?
3. What is one action you could take to listen better.

Feelings Keep Us Alive!

Almost every culture has rules about which emotions are okay to show in public. It even differs from school to school across America. Lots of happy people feel embarrassed if they show too much feeling in front of others. We learn these rules about hiding feelings from hearing people say things like, "Real men don't cry." Does that mean real men don't feel **sad?** I don't think so. I know I've felt happy and sad. I felt sad when my parents got divorced and happy, as they became happier. I've felt sad when someone I cared about was killed. Sadness, fear, anger, joy—all these feelings are natural and important. When we let ourselves feel our feelings, we own them. When we own them we can choose which feelings we want to keep and which we want to let go.

Another message a lot of us have learned is to pretend we're **happy** when we're not. Sayings like "Keep smiling!" or "Put on a happy face!" tell us to hide what we're really feeling behind a mask. Hiding behind pretend happiness is not the same as feeling real joy. **Joy** energizes us, makes us happy.

"Emotions Keep us alive."

We see things with fresh eyes. We're more optimistic; joy gives us a sense of power and ability. We can't just tell other people to be happy, but we can help them get there by caring about them.

With all these rules about how we're "supposed" to act in public, it would be easy to decide that emotions are bad. But that's not true. Emotions like fear, anger, sadness, and joy are an essential part of life. In fact, emotions keep us alive.

How does this work? **Feelings are messages from our brains and bodies that something has happened that we need to pay attention to in some way.**

Fear helps us to escape from or avoid danger. Anger is a signal that we feel someone or something is threatening us. **Anger** gets us ready to protect ourselves and stay alive. It makes us want to argue or fight and energizes us to attack. In times of real, physical danger, **anger** is the key to protecting the individual, the family and the community. Anger lets people know that their territory is being invaded, that something or someone important is being threatened. Anger can be a signal that it's time to protect ourselves. When we get angry, our bodies produce adrenaline, which speeds up our heart rate so our lungs and muscles can work together to get us out of danger. Feelings keep us alive. Thinking through our feelings helps us get what we need and stay connected with people we care about. *Managing our feelings helps us manage our lives.*

Action:

1. When were you last afraid?
2. When were you last angry?
3. Do you control your feelings, or do your feelings control you?

Being the Boss of Our Feelings

It's great that we have feelings to draw on when we really need them. But feelings sometimes get triggered when they're not needed, and that can be a problem. For instance, somebody may bump into someone in the hall and the person that was bumped gets really mad. But a bump in the hall is not really a dangerous situation. It may be *irritating*, or *frustrating*, but it doesn't really call for *anger*. And things only get worse when our egos get involved. Some schools understand this so well that they've made rules outlawing "fake" fighting. Other schools have started programs to help students learn to resolve arguments before they become fights.

Fear can make us freeze up or run away from situations that we really could handle if we stopped and thought about them. How many of us have gotten a headache or a stomach ache before an exam, or got stage *fright*, or *nerves* before a big game? This kind of fear is really *anxiety*, and it can stop us from doing our best. Sometimes we just don't speak out when we feel we should, and we feel bad about it later.

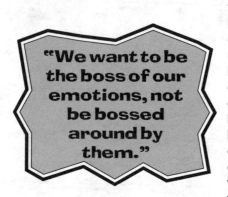

"We want to be the boss of our emotions, not be bossed around by them."

Sadness can help us deal with loss, but if we can't stop being sad, it swallows up our strength to do anything about it. Have you ever known another student who skipped school, stopped eating or hurt themselves because they were feeling sad that they weren't "good" enough or because they felt alone?

Joy is a great feeling. But some people, when they're not happy, turn to drugs, alcohol or life-threatening activities for thrills. These are not joy. They are a fake escape that makes returning to the real world even more difficult.

To be our own emotional boss, we need to do a few things. *First*, we need to feel what we are feeling; that is, to understand if *we're scared, sad, mad or glad*. *Second*, we need to take some time to figure out why we're feeling that way. What thoughts are we having that are making those emotions stronger? And *third*, we need to remember to give ourselves *time to cool down* when we're overcome by anger or fear. Only when we've cooled off some are we able to step into our peace keeper role and figure out the best action to take.

Young people can learn to manage their own emotions, and they can learn to help their friends manage their emotions, too. **We want to be the boss of our emotions, not be bossed around by them.**

Action

1. Have you ever been mad at something that later seemed unimportant?
2. How can you better control your feelings?
3. How could you help your friends better control their feelings?

Words Can Lead To Sticks And Stones

We've all heard the saying "Sticks and stones may break my bones but words will never hurt me." How wrong that can be! Words and information shape our views of the world and of ourselves. Bruises heal, broken bones mend stronger than before, but comments like, "You are never going to amount to anything!" can haunt us for years. Not only can words hurt, but with time and repetition, they can build up inside.

People our own age are especially good at using words that hurt. Maybe one of us is in a class and someone criticizes our paper or a question we ask, not knowing that we spent all weekend on that paper or couldn't hear the teacher. Maybe someone puts down our clothes or our hairstyle. Maybe they make a joke about our play in the big game, not realizing we felt bad already about what happened. Unintentional or thoughtless comments can really hurt, even if we try to ignore them.

The worst is when people say mean things on purpose. Words like, "You are too fat or too skinny, dumb, a nerd, a jock, or hopeless" can leave emotional bruises that take years to heal.

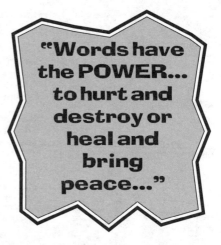

"Words have the POWER... to hurt and destroy or heal and bring peace..."

Usually people who feel deeply hurt let the other person know, although maybe not directly. For example, if a person's feelings are hurt, they may not answer or return another person's phone calls. They might ignore the person at school. They may say, "Oh no, nothing's bothering me." in a tone of voice that let's us know something is wrong, but not **what is wrong**. Some of us might feel so bad that, we believe those hurtful remarks. Some people may wait a long time to put someone down to get back at them, but people can have long memories about paybacks.

Some people don't realize how powerful their words can be until they hurt another badly. If someone says something hurtful to us, the first step to getting off the emotional roller-coaster *is not to take it personally*. We might want to take a step back, collect our thoughts, and then decide if it is worthwhile to continue the conversation. We might want to leave, just to cool off. Rather than a person feeling angry or ashamed they aren't perfect, or trying to keep the hurt to themselves, they might find someone they trust, and share with them how they feel. Letting our emotions take over only weakens us and strengthens the bully. In the worst cases, that's what they often want. They want us to get in a position where they're the winners, because *they see by our reaction that they hurt us.*

It's hard to overlook mean comments, gossip and jokes, because they hurt. Sometimes we need to let off steam alone or with others before we figure out if we need to do something else. The problem is, many people who are hurtful don't want to listen, because if they did, they'd have to admit we are people and have feelings. Often, they pretend to listen by saying, *"Hey, I didn't mean anything!"*, or even try to make us feel worse by saying things like "You can't take a joke," or *"What's your problem?"* and make fun of us even more.

People often say mean things because they hate the part of themselves they're putting down in someone else. Not liking yourself hurts, so mean people are usually in pain. They turn pain into anger and act out so other people will hurt too. This acting out can lead to acts of violence; in some cases, it leads to extreme violence.

That's where learning to be a *Peace Keeper* comes in. To end school violence, we need to protect ourselves and more. We must connect with others, especially those who are hurtful. It may not look like it, but they are the ones who need us the most.

Action:

1. Think about a time when someone said something that really hurt you?
2. How did you react?
3. What was the end result?

Peace Keepers:

Lead

Negotiation in Action

CORNERSTONE 3

– Peace Keepers: Stand Up For Each Other

Peace Keepers Look after Themselves and Each Other

Violence is a way to have power over other people. People who act out violently usually do it because they feel powerless. For whatever reasons—and there are many—these people are incredibly hurt and angry. In extreme cases, they try to manage that hurt and anger by scaring and hurting others. They do this to get revenge, sometimes on the people who hurt them or on groups that symbolize that hurt.

Our power lies not in hurtful words or actions, but in communication and caring. By working together—**by caring and connecting**—we can create safe school communities.

"Sometimes it's hard to act differently than the group we're in. It takes courage to stand up and be heard."

Many schools have responded to violence by making more rules and emergency management procedures and supervising everyone closely to enforce them. We can all understand why schools do this. They want us to be safe. We want to be safe. When we become Peace Keepers, we learn to supervise ourselves. We learn to create rules within ourselves that keep all of us safe. We live by them because we want to. And, if we work together to agree on those rules, it's far more likely that everyone will respect them.

Peace Keepers use their communication skills. They listen to each person or group's point of view. Peace Keepers respect people and expect to be respected in turn. With skill, we too can manage confrontation, anger, and fear. We can build a school where no one is so isolated or rejected that they resort to violence to show that they're "just as good" as anybody else.

Being a Peace Keeper means standing up for what we

believe. It means we don't agree with violence. It means backing up what we say by acting on our beliefs. This may mean stepping in to help negotiate a confrontation or walking away from a bad situation to stay safe. Action is the best way we can demonstrate that we live our beliefs.

As Peace Keepers, we can create a place where different people can listen and learn from each other, a place where people care about each other.

Action:

1. What are some of your school rules that are designed to prevent school violence?
2. Which of your school safety rules do you like?
3. What rules would you add or change to make your school safer?

Idea 21:

Taking Responsibility:
The Power of ONE

Each of us has the power to end school violence. But to do so, we must each take responsibility for our actions. We cannot change the past; *we can shape the future*. Our actions today can and will influence our world tomorrow. It's up to each us to decide what kind of influence we want to have. This book presents ideas and actions to help all of us become better at being who we already are—powerful people who can influence our school communities, take responsibility for our actions, and create a safer future. To make the ideas work, we must take the first step.

"We cannot change the past; we can shape the future. Our actions today can and will influence our world tomorrow."

Some people may think, "School violence doesn't have anything to do with me. I would never do anything to hurt other people." Is that really true? We all are part of our school community. *Every member* of our school community has the power to influence it. *That means each thing we do can potentially change our world, for better or worse.* This is a big idea. It means that even *one thing* that you or I do or say might change the way our school community interacts. With that much power comes a lot of responsibility. It's up to each one of us to decide what we can do to end school violence. Let's start our actions with understanding.

Tragic school violence doesn't just explode out of nowhere. Small acts of violence, like ignoring someone, bullying, harsh words and mean looks, pave the way for bigger acts of violence. When violence gets more out of hand, things can get destroyed, fights can break out, and in extreme cases, terrible things can happen.

But there's another side to the situation. That's the *Power of One.* It's the power that each of us has to change things.

We can listen. We can respect other people's viewpoints. We can respect our own feelings and abilities. We can decide not to take part in group talk that is harmful and not helpful to other people. We can help people manage big emotions, like anger. We can give them some ideas about how to deal with their problems. In tense situations, we can help stop arguments or alienation from building into disasters.

It's up to us to see the early signs of violence around us. And it's up to us to decide what each and every one of us can do about it. We need to begin to use our "power of one" to make a difference. We have to see and understand violence at all levels in order to end it.

Action:

1. Have you ever seen violence within your school community?
2. How did the violence stop?
3. Did you feel different after seeing violence at your own school?

Self-criticism Can Hurt

We need to be **Peace Keepers on the Inside.** We are surrounded by information, images, and advertisements that come in a multitude of formats. This ongoing flow of information has a big impact on how many of us feel about ourselves. When we stand in a checkout line, we can't help but see all the popular magazines covered with photos of the latest teen idols. Their headlines shout to us about money, cars, expensive vacations, and how we too can look perfect if we only try hard enough. They seem to show that you can't be popular unless you're thin, unless you're tall, unless you're buff.

TV shows and the commercials that pay for them, do the same thing. You won't be loved unless you wear the right vest, the right sneakers, and the right designer labels. People who "make it" have expensive cars and don't seem to ever really go to work. Characters in sitcoms spend all their time talking about who's dating whom and making smart remarks about each other. Did you ever notice that people on TV often aren't very nice to each other? And almost everyone on those shows looks perfect. Perfect hair, perfect shape, perfect teeth. I don't know about you, but I was never perfect and I never will be. But I am quite happy with myself.

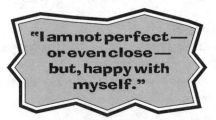

"I am not perfect — or even close — but, happy with myself."

Did you know that the average American child sees over 250,000 TV commercials by the time they're ten years old? Wow! That's a lot of information telling us what we have to buy and do and be in order to be happy! This endless parade of perfect TV stars and razzle-dazzle commercials urging us to buy, buy, buy can result in some people accepting these values as real, and some people judging others only on how they look and what they own.

The saddest part is that sometimes, when people judge us, a few of us start to believe it's true. We start to believe that we lack something, or that we don't have what it takes to succeed. Some of us tell ourselves we're failures, or hate ourselves because someone has told us we're too tall or too thin or too fat or too short. These critical thoughts can cause us to feel hurt and angry.

Action:

1. Do you know anyone that always puts himself or herself down?
2. Do you ever put yourself down?
3. Do you feel better or worse afterwards?

Peace Making with Yourself:
Liking the Self You are Becoming

We all know criticism can hurt. But have you noticed that sometimes our own thoughts can hurt us too? This is important: thoughts can create feelings. If I think to myself, "My arms are way too skinny," I feel bad, because I'm seeing myself through a filter of criticism. That's like putting on a pair of sunglasses that only let me see what *I don't like* about myself.

What if we put on sunglasses that improve our vision of ourselves—that help us to see what's good and strong and beautiful in us? This is easier to say than do. Habits are hard to break, and the habit of self-criticism can be strong. I knew someone who, when she made a mistake, always said to herself, "What's wrong with me?" And then guess what? She felt terrible! You know why? Her question began with the idea that there was already something wrong with her and her job was to find out what it was this time. Ouch! She was asking the wrong question. The more negative we are about ourselves, the worse we make ourselves feel. This is a common thing that many athletes do. When things are not going their way, they start blaming themselves and saying negative things to themselves. World class athletes don't blame themselves; they look instead at what they can do better, and then they encourage themselves to do it.

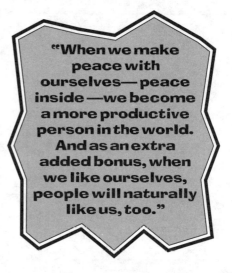

"When we make peace with ourselves— peace inside —we become a more productive person in the world. And as an extra added bonus, when we like ourselves, people will naturally like us, too."

What if, when we make a mistake, we ask instead, "What did I do right? What can I do next?" This is a much better response. It says that the situation can be changed, and we have the power to improve it. What a great realization. If any of us don't like parts of ourselves, we can just ask: "Is there anything that I can do to change this?" If there is and the solution keeps us healthy, then go for it! But what if you don't like something about yourself that you can't change, like your height? What do you do then? That's where peace-making with yourself comes in. Everybody has things about themselves that are different from other people. The question is, can you learn to like what's unique and special about you? The alternative—hating yourself for the rest of your life—is not much fun. Until we learn to love and appreciate ourselves, it's hard for others, too.

Being proud of all of yourself is a big step, especially for young people. We don't have to be conditioned by outside influences to think that there is only **ONE** way to be strong or beautiful. There are a million ways. And we can start seeing the strength or the beauty in each of us by focusing on what's right about us, and by owning what's special. Turn away criticism or transform it into something positive.

When we make peace with ourselves—peace inside— we become a more productive person in the world. And, as an extra added bonus, when we like ourselves, people will naturally like us, too. When we like ourselves, our energy isn't pulled into managing hurt and depression and anger. Instead, it's freed up to help each of us be the best person we can be and to be a *Peace Keeper* in our school community. If you can become a *Peace Keeper* on the inside, you can share it on the outside.

Action:

1. Do you like yourself?
2. Do you think other people like you?
3. How could you feel better about yourself?

Idea 24:

Know the Danger Signs

The top three causes of death in young people—car accidents, homicide, and suicide—are all related to violence. Car accidents often happen when people drive recklessly or under the influence of drugs or alcohol, or take out their anger in road rage. Homicides happen when people don't know how to manage hurt, anger, and other feelings. They take it out on other people. And suicide happens when people turn hurt and anger inside on themselves.

These statistics are not acceptable. It is ridiculous that our nation's young people should die from violence. Our lives are much too precious for any of these things to happen. All of these cases can be stopped. To end school violence, we must first learn to recognize its signs.

Stop Sign:
Reckless Driving

Never get in a car with someone who you think is going to drive irresponsibly, and let someone else drive if you feel you cannot drive safely.

If you notice any of these signs, it's better to get a ride home with someone else. If at all possible, keep the driver who is impaired from driving—even if you have to take the keys.

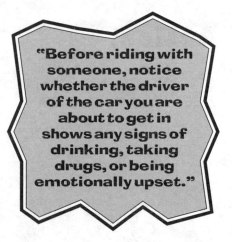

"Before riding with someone, notice whether the driver of the car you are about to get in shows any signs of drinking, taking drugs, or being emotionally upset."

Sadly, many of my friends have been killed or severely injured in car accidents. Even one person hurt is too many, especially if it's someone you care about. Rarely do I speak at a school where an auto tragedy has not occurred in recent memory. Some people may feel invincible behind the wheel of a car, but they and the innocent people they kill are not invincible. Driving recklessly shatters more than glass.

Never drive angry. Take the time you need to cool down or help the driver to cool down. A speeding car is not the vehicle for expressing anger, it's just bad outcomes waiting to happen.

Action:

1. Has anyone you know been hurt in a car accident because of alcohol, drugs, or reckless driving?
2. How did you feel when it happened?
3. What could have been done to prevent the accident?

Stop Sign:
Hurting Other People

Some people think that dressing wildly or differently is the first sign to look for in someone who might want to hurt you. This is not necessarily true. Sometimes, people like to get creative with the way they look, use their hair or their clothes to make a statement. ***Being different does not equal being dangerous.*** It's not what people look like that lets us know they're potentially dangerous— it's what they do. It's their behaviors.

"Being different does not equal being dangerous, It's not what people look like that lets us know they're potentially dangerous— it's what they do. It's their behaviors."

One of the first behavior signs to look for is resentment and prejudice against others. Hate has real potential to lead to violence. Does someone show that they actively hate a person or group? That may mean they feel like a victim, like someone is trying to put them down or be "better" than they are. They use hate to make themselves feel more important. Sometimes it may also mean that they want to feel superior by saying that other groups are inferior. Either way, this kind of superior/inferior view creates problems that may lead to violence. Do other people bully or actually hurt people? Do they destroy property, say mean or threatening things, brag about having weapons, or carry weapons? These are important signs to look for. People who make threats may carry them out. Most places where threats or violence occur are areas that no one person exactly "owns". School hallways, parking lots and alleyways are common places. If you hear someone threatening or bullying someone else, get together with people you trust to talk it over. Getting more than one person's ideas can help you better figure out what you might want to do. Then you can plan better what steps to take next.

Other behaviors may be less obvious. Does a person pull away from the group, look sad or angry or expressionless most of the time? This may mean that they are feeling separated from the group and feel sad or angry about it. However, if someone likes to stay alone, don't automatically assume they're dangerous and start treating them like they're trouble. They may just be shy or waiting for someone to talk to them. Be a real **Peace Keeper**. Talk to them and see if you can get to know them, begin to explore the uniqueness they can bring to the school community. If you think someone is in danger of hurting other people, tell a responsible adult. The key is to be alert and share your concern with an adult you trust.

Some people can be prone to violence because of mental illness. Sometimes, these problems can be healed with modern-day medicine. But sometimes people don't know they're ill. If you notice people talking aloud about strange things that don't seem to make sense, or maybe even talking about hurting other people, talk this over with an adult you trust. Teachers or counselors can help most in these cases. But behavior like this is no joke: it's serious. People who are having mental difficulty deserve respect and help, not teasing and name calling. If you really notice that someone seems to be having problems or talking about hurting other people, take action. Talk about it with someone you trust.

Action:

1. Do you know anyone that has threatened to hurt someone?
2. Are you worried that they are serious?
3. Who could you tell?

Stop Sign:
People Might Hurt Themselves

Everyone has times when they are sad - that's normal. Life isn't always easy, and no one gets everything they want. There are times when each of us fails to make the grade, make the team, win the award. Sadness is a normal part of life, but most people bounce back after a few hours, a day or two, or even a month if it's severe.

People who are depressed don't bounce back. Major depression is like a gray fog that doesn't lift, no matter how hard the person tries to lift it. It takes away hope and makes it hard just getting from day to day. This is the depression that can lead to people toward harming themselves.

Another behavior that adds to depression is thinking that bad things are going to happen in the future. When someone thinks that the future is bleak, that nothing good can happen, they feel terrible. The truth is, none of us knows what the future holds. But purely negative thoughts just spiral down into more bad thoughts and depression.

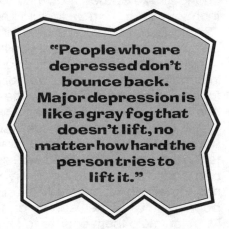

"People who are depressed don't bounce back. Major depression is like a gray fog that doesn't lift, no matter how hard the person tries to lift it."

There is a strong connection between negative thoughts and feeling bad, just as there is between positive thoughts and feeling good.

Sometimes people who are struggling with depression have trouble with sleep. They may sleep all the time or never be able to sleep. They may have a lot of nightmares, or wake up in the middle of the night, worried and anxious. They may feel helpless to change this because depression and anxiety or worry is eating away at their peace of mind.

People who feel seriously depressed may tend to isolate themselves, stay away from others or lock themselves in their rooms. One of the clearest signs that a person is in danger of hurting themselves is if they talk about how worthless their life is or how they might as well be dead. They may take steps to plan for how they would kill themselves.

Pay attention. Suicide is not a joke. It could be the end of a friend's life. Don't pretend this kind of "joke" is funny. If a person talks about suicide, the first thing to ask them is if they mean it. Then listen closely to that person's answer and let them talk about how they feel. If they are serious, or even halfway serious, help them to find the help they need. In ninth grade, a friend from my English class attempted suicide. It was so scary. There were so many signs, yet everyone—including me—chose not to see them. She lived, thankfully, and today is doing great. And now, *I pay attention* because I never want to see that happen again.

Sometimes people who are really angry don't know what to do with their anger, so they take it out on themselves. They may cut themselves with razor blades, or burn themselves with cigarettes. They do this because they are hurting so badly that pain seems like a normal part of life. They might starve themselves or overeat, binge and throw up, drink or take drugs. They may do this to try to make the pain go away. It is also a way to take control in a situation that is awful but cannot be changed, like abuse. They may say horrible, hurtful things to themselves, like "I am so stupid! I'll never amount to anything."

Sadly, self-destructive behaviors don't make the pain go away. They make it worse. If you hear a friend talking about suicide, saying hateful words about themselves or revealing information about physical abuse: listen. Then suggest asking for help or calling a help line. *The National Violence Hotline number is 1-800-799-SAFE.*

If the friend does not seem suicidal and doesn't seem depressed or self-abusive, you may be able to help them by telling them about the good you see in them. Positive thinking can lead to positive feeling. Everyone—every single person—has something wonderful to offer in this world. Help other people find what they can do and contribute in the world. It just might help them choose to stay alive.

Action:

1. Do you know anyone that might be depressed?
2. Have you talked with them about it?
3. Have you shared your concern with an adult you trust?

Asking For Help:
"Help! I'm Drowning In Life!"

Asking for help from other people can be hard. Maybe pride keeps some of us from asking, or maybe we just don't know how to ask. Perhaps we think we'll be rejected if we ask someone to lend us a hand or teach us what they know. Maybe we feel that if we ask someone for their support we'll have to do what they say. We may wonder if other people will think we're odd if we ask for help.

All of us need help at some time in our lives. Needing help from others can happen to anyone, not just youth. Education leaders, political leaders, scientists, athletes all get help sometimes. That's what makes them successful—recognizing that they don't know everything, but they can find someone who knows what they need at that moment. Everyone needs guidance and belief at some point in their life, and one of the best ways to move forward when we're stuck is to simply ask for help.

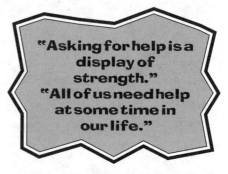

"Asking for help is a display of strength."
"All of us need help at some time in our life."

Asking for help is a display of strength. It shows confidence, because it takes a confident person to feel strong enough to admit there are things he or she doesn't know. It takes the most courage when in a group because we may feel pressured not to ask, to hide our weakness from others. Nobody is born knowing everything. People need help to learn all kinds of things, like how to drive a car, tie a tie, cook, or cope with the grief they feel when someone they care about has died. In the end, the person who can ask for help will go much farther in life than the one who tries to do it all alone. Why? The more we ask, the more we learn, the more people are willing to help, and the more people we can help.

If you are not sure what you can do immediately to deal with challenges in your life, ask someone you trust for help. The worst they can say is "no," which is a good answer, because it just means that someone else is better suited to help you. If one person can't help, keep asking until you find someone who can. Asking for help is a true sign of strength.

Action:

1. Who would you ask for academic help at school?
2. Who would you ask for help with a personal problem?
3. Have you ever asked anyone for help?

Managing the Emotions
That Can Lead to Violence

Violence often happens because people get emotionally carried away and act before they stop to think. We learned earlier how important feelings are to our safety. Even emotions that we may have thought were bad—like fear and anger—are actually a vital part of how we keep ourselves safe and alive. Feelings in themselves aren't bad, but unmanaged emotions sometimes cause people to behave in ways that are bad.

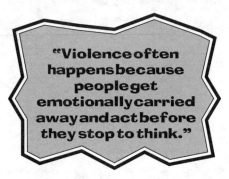

"Violence often happens because people get emotionally carried away and act before they stop to think."

When we are angry, we may act in ways that can cause worse problems than what made us angry to begin with.

Acting emotionally—without thinking—can lead to violence in our schools, communities, and the world. It's not feelings that do the damage; the damage comes from reactions that sometimes arise from the feelings. To end school violence, we all have to become feeling managers, and here are the steps to doing that.

9 Steps to Managing Feelings:

1. <u>Notice your feelings</u> -talk to someone you trust if you are confused about them.
2. <u>Cool down when you are upset</u> -go to a different place if you need to.
3. <u>Separate real emergencies</u> -decide if it's urgent or an emotional false alarm.
4. <u>Walk away</u> -if you feel out-of-control or in danger.
5. <u>Deal with real emergencies</u> -find a safe place and someone that you can talk to openly.
6. <u>Make plans</u>-create an action plan to deal with the dilemma.

7. <u>Find help</u> -a parent, friend, counselor, teacher, etc. may be able to help you.
8. <u>Be a Peace Keeper</u> -lead.
9. <u>Practice the steps</u> -of the Peace Keeping process

Peace Making In Emergency Situations:

Our generation can no longer allow violence. We must start by making examples in our own lives. Violence is not entertaining or productive. When a young person dies from a fight that escalated needlessly, something could have been done to prevent or end it. We can act to save ourselves and each other.

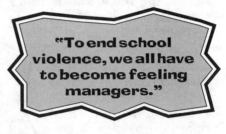

"To end school violence, we all have to become feeling managers."

1) Don't get swept away, even though you may feel angry or afraid.
2) Get away and get help.
3) Take others away with you.
4) Stay calm.
5) Use a verbal or straight talker strategy if you can.
6) Realize people may not listen.
7) Defend yourself physically only in extreme emergency.
8) Above all, don't react to false alarms by striking or lashing out verbally.

Action:

1. Have you ever been in a real emergency?
2. How did you feel and act during the emergency?
3. What was the end result of your actions?

End Violence Before it Begins:
Work the Steps in the Peace Keeping Process

The goal of peace-keeping is to prevent confrontations from becoming violent. **Peace Keepers** use both **Team Player** and **Straight Talker** skills to mediate or resolve the situation.

These skills are vital to keep a potentially bad situation from getting out of control. As amazingly effective as adults can be in ending our confrontation, having one of our peers help can generate powerful results. Knowing what it's like to be a student and possibly some of the involved students' background, we can often relate well to both sides. We, as students,

"As amazingly effective as adults can be in ending our confrontation, having one of our peers help can generate powerful results."

usually have little direct power over the students involved, **so how** we handle the situation is critical to resolving the confrontation. We deal with issues as peers and can use the respect of being a peer to influence a positive result to disagreements. Here are some basic steps to ending a disagreement before it gets ugly:

1. ASSESS
Determine if the situation is safe for you to intervene. If there is a threat of immediate physical danger to you or other people, find someone who can safely end the confrontation.

2. ENGAGE
If you can safely intervene, ask each side if they want to resolve the confrontation. Intervening will only work if both sides agree to work towards a solution. If they will not agree to work towards a solution, it may be best to give both sides time to get their emotions in control so they can rationally resolve the issue later.

3. SHARE

With one student sharing at a time, let each side share why they are arguing. Sometimes this may solve the situation simply because one person misinterpreted the other person. Make it clear each person involved will get their own turn to share their version. Be careful not to let one side cut the other one off or make unnecessary comments.

4. CREATE

After each person involved has shared their version of events and why they disagree, let each side create possible solutions. Let each person submit a solution and then let them discuss what is best. If necessary, keep both sides on track and from getting emotional over their personal solution.

5. SOLVE

After discussing what can work best for everyone, let the group select an outcome. If a win-win solution is possible, get everyone to agree before ending the discussion. If one clear solution is not possible, let the group decide if they should take time to discuss the disagreement later. Depending on the result, either set another time for them to talk things out or go with the group solution.

Action:

1. If you saw a violent fight, what would you do?
2. What peace keeper skill do you think is more important?
3. If it was a simple disagreement instead of a fight, how could you help resolve it?

Idea 28:

Drugs And Alcohol:
The HIGHway To Failure

For my generation, the eternal symbol of a brain on drugs will be a frying egg. Growing up, people were always telling me how bad drugs and alcohol were and how they could keep me from reaching my goals. I never quite understood that until now.

Every one of my friends in high school had tremendous potential. Every single one! It didn't matter whether they were smart, popular, class clowns, athletic, a bit rebellious, or a combination of all five—they all had something great to offer in the world. But recently, after graduating from high school, I began noticing changes in my friends. Subtle things, like some of the super-cool people from high school weren't the ones who found jobs or became popular at college. Friends I knew my entire life suddenly were not close. Everyone seemed to get busier as they became more responsible and independent. But the biggest change I've seen has been in people who've gotten involved with drugs and alcohol. Drugs and alcohol are easy to get, and some of my friends took the bait.

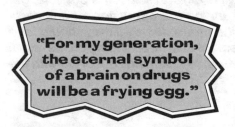

"For my generation, the eternal symbol of a brain on drugs will be a frying egg."

The short-term impact of their using was not too dramatic: a few missed classes, a drop in grades, a change in attitude. Yet now when I talk with them It feels like much of their excitement about life and hope for the future has dimmed. They are no longer the people I hung out with, shared experiences with, and looked forward to seeing. Drugs and alcohol have changed them.

Drugs and alcohol lower inhibitions, loosen our ability to take care of ourselves. When we can't care for ourselves, people may take advantage of us, tense situations may get out of control, and we might do things we normally wouldn't do. All of these situations hurt; they hurt us and they hurt those we love. A few of the people I grew up with have overdosed or been arrested for drug possession. Several have been killed in drinking and driving accidents, and many others have a terrible look of hopelessness in their eyes.

Watching them, I have felt helpless too. I feel sad when I think of them, because I wonder if there was something I could've done to help them, like maybe telling them that I cared as they began to tumble backwards. Recently, I took a stand with a friend, told her that I was deeply concerned about her drinking. Starting that conversation was hard. I felt awkward and clumsy, but I also knew I had to speak. I couldn't live with myself if I didn't take some responsibility for a person I cared about.

After I talked with my friend, she contacted someone who could help her, and talked to people who were in recovery from drinking and using drugs. They gave her the understanding and the support that she needed to go for help herself.

Sometimes we need help to get help. It can be hard to ask for support, admit we have an addiction, be open to other people's advice, but sometimes it's absolutely necessary. It doesn't take much to get us off course, and the longer we're off course, the harder it is to get back on. Drugs and alcohol cause young people to lose their focus, change their priorities, forget their dreams, and even die. To end the self-inflicted violence of drug and alcohol use, we need to be responsible for our own actions. Please don't let drugs and alcohol ruin your life or the lives of others. Find a place to get help.

Action:

1. Do you know anyone using drugs?
2. Have you talked to them about ending their drug use?
3. What would you or did you say?

Idea 29:

Integrating Differences:
Building School Communities That Work

I've shared in earlier sections about the importance of not getting stuck in an "I'm better than you are" attitude. This is an incredibly narrow and incorrect view. It's a view that cements divisions between "us" and "them," whoever us and them are. This kind of snobbism is a recipe for unhappiness and isolation.

How can each student in a school find a way to value what is unique and special about every person in the school community? Here's how we can begin.

Groups come together most often because the people in them are similar. It's easy to be around people who are like us. It's comfortable to share the same view of the world, and we don't have to work hard to get along when our opinions are all similar. Groups tend to separate when the members find it difficult to manage differences. If someone is too small, weird, smart, dumb, whatever, the group has a tendency to scapegoat them. Scapegoat is a very old term. In ancient cultures, it was a live goat over whose head were confessed all the sins of the tribe; then the goat was sent away into the wilderness, carrying the sins of the group with it. In a community, a scapegoat is a person or group rejected by the main culture, labeled icky or scary or gross, and cast out because people can't bear to be around their differences. Then everyone in the main group gets to feel superior to those cast out, and no one has to feel responsible for talking to the "out" group, because everyone agrees they're too weird. People scapegoat because the person they are rejecting has the very trait that they cannot bear in themselves.

But what happens to the scapegoats? Some of them lead lonely, isolated lives. Some of them kill themselves. Some of them grow up to be the most creative of us all. And some of

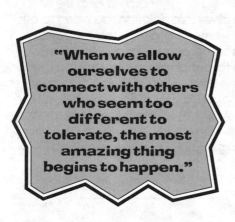

"When we allow ourselves to connect with others who seem too different to tolerate, the most amazing thing begins to happen."

them get so angry that all they care about is getting even. What an incredible waste of human potential.

But there is a solution. It's not an easy solution, because it requires all of us—every single one of us—to step out of our comfort zones and connect with other people. If your school were to create one single, over-riding goal, it might look something like this:

To create strong connections, communication, and trust between all school community members.

The national organization that I work with is called **YouthConnect** because basically, its goal is for everyone to better connect with each other. When we allow ourselves to connect with others who seem too different to tolerate, the most amazing thing begins to happen. What seem to be intolerable differences start to fade. People begin to realize that everyone wants to love and be loved, create and be recognized, contribute and be valued. And people contribute in the most amazing and unexpected ways. **YouthConnect** is devoted to bringing our generation of young people together and being a voice for our needs.

Action:

1. Join **YouthConnect** at *www.endschoolviolence.com*
2. Start or join a youth organization at your school.
3. Work to find creative ways to bring your school together.

Idea 30:

School Safety Begins With Trust

Ending school violence requires trust. Trust requires open, honest communication. If we trust one another and feel safe in a school community, we can become its **Peace Keepers**. In a safe school, we can learn more and have fun doing it. When we communicate clearly from a community perspective, we can solve problems before things get out of control. In working with young people of every background across the country, I've heard a lot of people say they have trouble trusting other people. Too often I hear "I don't trust anyone," "I have no one I can talk to and trust with my feelings," or "I feel like I am in this all alone."

"Once we are defensive, we stop trusting and start ignoring."

Lack of trust stops communication. When we can't communicate, we feel isolated and alone. The more alone we feel, the more unpro-tected and vulnerable we feel. The more vulnerable we feel, the more we fear for ourselves and our survival in the world. Even if we have a few friends, we can still feel alone because we don't have support from the larger community. Lack of trust creates a cycle of bad results.

Trust is hard to build and easy to break. Sometimes, though, we must learn to forgive if our trust is broken. The ability to build and rebuild trust is critical for good relationships. Friendships, partnerships and agreements depend on trust. With trust we show we believe both in ourselves and in other people. We trust people who honor their agreements and distrust those who don't. Our ability to keep or not keep commitments can be our greatest strength or worst weakness.

There are many levels of trust, and we trust different people with different areas of our lives.

When trust is broken, how we react depends on who broke our trust, why they did it, how hurt we felt. Sometimes other people make mistakes that we feel hurt by. Sometimes we break trust with someone we know. When that happens, we have to see if we can forgive or be forgiven. None of us is perfect, and it's unrealistic to expect perfection from ourselves or others. We can all learn in some area, no matter what our age. Building trust is a learning experience for everyone.

Trust is sometimes difficult for us to build. Perhaps we are fearful of building trust because our trust was broken in the past. Our trust may be broken, but we cannot let our spirit break. It's important to learn from bad experiences, not let them limit our lives. Trust and straight talk will make us stronger as individuals and will help our community to end school violence. If we all found one person outside our normal group of influence to talk with each day, and sincerely tried to build shared trust, then no one would feel as alone or excluded. That's real community commitment.

Action:

1. Who do you trust most at school?
2. What could you do that would help you to trust more people?
3. What could you do to have more people trust you?

Empathy and Apologies

To end school violence and build safe school communities, we have to do more than be **Peace Keepers** during emergencies. We also have to do maintenance—do peacekeeping behaviors in times of peace. It's just like taking care of a car; if you want it to run, you change the oil. If you want clean clothes, you do the laundry. Real **Peace Keepers** work at it every day, and one of the ways they do this is by developing empathy skills.

What is empathy anyway? Empathy is an important word. It means understanding and recognizing other people's strong emotions, especially hurt and anger. When people get their feelings hurt, it helps them to know that someone else understands and cares. One way to show we care is to tell them we're sorry that they're hurting.

This doesn't mean we have to take the blame for their hurt. Sometimes we may have caused the hurt; if that's the case, then we need to take the blame. And we apologize. Other times, we may not have intended to hurt them. When this happens, we can still apologize for their being in pain. We can say, "I'm sorry that you're hurting or upset." That's empathy—understanding how hard it is to hurt. If we want people to care about us, we need to show we care about them.

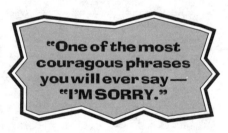

"One of the most couragous phrases you will ever say— "I'M SORRY."

We all make mistakes, disappoint people, and just plain mess up at some point in our lives. I make mistakes all the time, and I work to learn from each one. I try not to make the same mistake twice, especially if it hurts someone. I can feel hurt for a lot of reasons: if I sprain my ankle, if somebody special forgets my birthday, if something happens to my family. But that doesn't mean the other person actually tried to hurt me.

Probably the greatest lesson I've learned from making tons of mistakes is to apologize—immediately, sincerely and profusely. It's the best way to begin resolving any mistake. Apologize, share what you have learned, and decide what you will do to make sure it will not happen again.

The worst thing we can do is fail to apologize and hope time will mend all wounds. Time does not necessarily heal. Sometimes our pride can be a barrier; and admitting we are wrong may feel like humiliation when actually it is a strength. People respect honesty and know that we are going to make mistakes; so take time to apologize and learn from the experience. If we could get more people to apologize instead of allowing pride to control their actions, we could avert school violence through peaceful resolutions. The ability to apologize is a tremendous strength and brings people together.

Action:

1. Have you ever hurt someone's feelings?
2. How did you resolve the hurt?
3. Would you do anything differently now?

Idea 32:

Forgiveness

Whenever someone breaks our trust, hurts us, or fails to meet our expectations, forgiveness can be difficult. The greater our disappointment, the harder it is to forgive. Until we forgive the person who broke our trust, we cannot repair the relationship and begin learning from the experience.

If you truly want to help the person who broke your trust, the greatest thing you can do is **forgive them. Forgiveness is the key to moving forward.** When someone makes a sincere effort to apologize, accept his or her apology, and offer forgiveness.

Several times in my life, close friends have disappointed me or broken commitments I held dear. Each time it hurt, and I wanted to end the friendship or find fault with the friend. After finding an outlet for my emotion, usually talking through the incident with a mentor or other friend, I found myself willing to forgive them and wanting to rebuild our relationship.

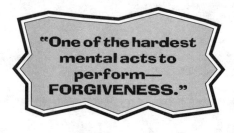

"One of the hardest mental acts to perform— FORGIVENESS."

Even if someone does not apologize to you, forgive him or her. They may not have the courage to apologize; they may not know how badly you were hurt. Forgive them anyway. Sharing your forgiveness is the best thing you can do to rebuild trust, even if they don't apologize. If someone continually violates your trust, it may be time to end that friendship. If they don't respect you, it can hurt you in the long run.

To end school violence we must stop holding grudges and begin forgiving so we can repair relationships.

Action:

1. Has someone hurt your feelings recently?
2. Did they apologize when they hurt you?
3. Did you or could you forgive them?

Idea 33:

Finding Your Life Purpose and Planning for Success

In our quest to meet our daily responsibilities, the bigger picture can become blurred or even non-existent.

Remembering that we have a larger purpose than just schoolwork, jobs, chores, and energy consuming activities is a key for life-long success. This can be complicated when we do not clearly know our purpose or how to begin to find it.

One thing I've learned is that material things, such as cars, houses, and other "things" that are so often seen as success, truly do not bring lasting fulfillment. I know a number of very wealthy people who would trade all their money for a loving family, some good friends, and the knowledge that someone truly cares about them. Unfortunately, in our quest for financial success, it can take us too long to realize that money isn't actually everything, and all the advice we received early in our lives to the contrary, was not quite true.

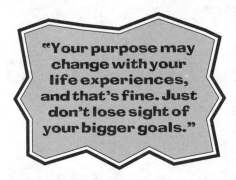

"Your purpose may change with your life experiences, and that's fine. Just don't lose sight of your bigger goals."

I have learned from my mentors that many people get so caught in the endless cycle of pursuing money that they misuse their scarcest resource—time. Money does not outlive us; it just goes to someone else. Only what we do to help others truly lasts. A life purpose is something greater than money, greater than even ourselves; it is a selfless explanation of why we live. As an example, my life purpose is to build powerful people, families, and communities who inspire, influence, and improve our world. Simple, and direct. **This life purpose makes every decision I make in life much easier.** All I do is make choices that are most in line with my life purpose. The following questions can make every choice simple: By participating in a certain activity am I practicing what I teach? Is this choice in line with my life purpose? Did I do everything possible to help that person?

Your purpose may change with your life experiences, and that's fine. Just don't lose sight of your bigger goals. As more people create a selfless purpose and commit to improving the world, we will move forward to ending school violence.

Action:

1. What is your life purpose?
2. Has it changed in the last three years?
3. Have you told anyone your life purpose?

Idea 34:

Praise and the Power of Expectations

People enjoy praise. How about a compliment for when we've put a lot of energy into doing a good job? When we've done the best we can or when we've worked with effort to finish a project, praise feels good. Often, we try hard to reach our own goals or help someone else, and being recognized is rewarding. We deserve praise for working with all our heart, for throwing ourselves into a task, whether it's raking leaves or fixing a car. It's even nice to hear praise for caring about our family, friends, and school community.

We also deserve praise for reaching our goals.

"The greatest gift that we can provide someone is sincere belief in him or her. Especially when it's for something they really value."

Sometimes we're happy with what we make or the results we get. For example, it's always a relief when we make a decent grade on a big test, or make good on a promise. When we meet our savings goals, paint a picture or learn a new song on the guitar, we feel successful and good. It's especially wonderful to be complimented for what we love and value about ourselves that others rarely notice.

Although many of us feel shy about it, almost all of us like to be praised.

Sometimes its confusing when people praise us for things we have—like cars, houses, nice eyes or thick hair. We're not those things, but many of us mix up who we are with compliments about how we look or what we own. Maybe we deserve praise for the hard work of saving to buy a CD player. But praise for the CD player is not really a compliment about us—it's a compliment for a thing. People are much more than what they own or don't own. People are much more than their looks. People are what's inside.

Praise only works if we mean what we say. Fake praise never works. Did you know that body movements, facial expression, and the way our voice sounds make up **93%** of the message we communicate when we talk? Only **7%** of the message comes from the actual words! Tone of voice or body movements can show when people don't mean what they say. It's useless to praise people in a way that actually puts them down. For example, telling someone that their hair would be cool *if only it* was a better color, longer, or curlier is a subtle way of saying their hair is not okay the way it is.

There's yet another benefit to telling others we admire them. This is the **power of expectations**. If we notice what people do well, we see them as life winners. Life winners always are growing and learning: they are positive about themselves. Support and praise from others helps our confidence grow. This is one of the reasons many of us ask for compliments like, "How do you feel about my paper?" Praise helps us know we're on the right track and gives us the courage to go on.

If we want to ask someone to change their behavior, we need to first focus on what that person does well. Let's say they have fantastic ideas or are a great team player. Tell them about that. This puts both us and the other person in a positive mind set. Our praise tells them how working with them has been good for us all. Then we can go on to talk about the habit we would like them to change. When we focus on what people do well, the big problem turns into a smaller one, and the person we've talked to understands our needs. Then we can work together to find solutions.

Praise helps people feel good and brings communities together.

Action:

1. What is the best praise you have ever received? How did it make you feel?
2. Who was it from?
3. Did you praise anyone today?

Serving Leaders

Great people commit themselves to serving other people. Good leaders manage people to meet goals. **Great leaders** commit themselves to helping the people they serve to become as strong and skilled as they can be to reach these goals. Great leaders treat people as equals, no matter who they are: it's only our jobs or abilities that are different, not our essential value as people.

A leader raises people's spirits and inspires them to do their best. We trust great leaders. They expect us to do the best we can do, and they care about and try to serve our needs, too. If a favorite older person we know is a leader, chances are they are also a source of support and a teacher of some aspect of life. Anybody can be a great leader, from the homemaker on your block to a grocery clerk or the president of a huge company.

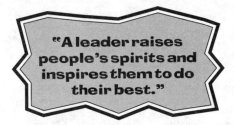

"A leader raises people's spirits and inspires them to do their best."

One sign of a leader is that he or she doesn't need to control all of a job or project. Especially in large companies, a leader may handle higher-level duties and be a coach to help people stay on track. No one needs people yelling at them, but most people like encouragement and support. In a well-led group, everyone contributes, and a leader trusts that everyone will do what they need to do. When people work as a team, responsibilities are shared, and people support each other.

Sometimes we feel like we are only one person, so we can't make an impact. This is not true. Every great movement in history started with just one person. When people embrace a powerful goal, they begin to see how they can help turn that goal into reality. Then the movement spreads. Perhaps it becomes a permanent part of our culture, like an America where everyone can be equal.

If we can help others in **any** way, we can change our community. By working with great leaders in our community, we can put our skills to work and learn new ones. We can serve others and serve ourselves at the same time.

Action:

1. Who is a leader that you respect?
2. Why do you respect them?
3. What qualities do you and this leader have in common?

Transition Means Change

Life is full of transitions. During our high school years, we must adjust almost constantly to change. But in a way, life is one long transition. We are all constantly learning and growing. Ending school violence now is a change that will affect us for the rest of our lives.

When life sends us off in a new direction, we may doubt our ability to change and interact with new people. Transitional periods are stressful, even when the changes are good. Think about the time we're most unsure about how we fit in to our new situation—usually the very beginning. The highest dropout rate for high schools, colleges, technical programs, and other training programs is the first year. The year we learn to drive a car is when we tend to have the most accidents. The first year we work at a job can be tense, especially if we need to learn and earn money to make ends meet. Then there's dealing with the physical and emotional changes of maturing, and the mental stretch of getting a good education.

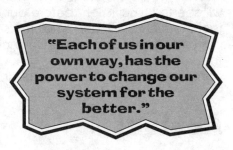

"Each of us in our own way, has the power to change our system for the better."

Change can make us feel stressed to the max, overwhelmed with expectations, or just frustrated with all that is occurring. To reduce this stress, we must begin by taking care of ourselves. We need some time for ourselves every day. Friends who give us support and trust can listen to our experiences and give us feedback on our feelings. Mentors and coaches help us make sense of life's challenges. A healthy lifestyle, with enough sleep and a balanced diet, will help us feel energetic, strong, flexible and coordinated.

But sometimes, all this pressure can build up. That's why violence of almost all types is higher in teens and other young adults than in any other section of the population. Quite a few of us have already seen explosions of raw emotions or violence. Maybe it's in high school hallways, maybe it's vandalism of property, maybe it's in the self-destruction of a friend.

The first few weeks or months of a movement to end

school violence will be a time of great uncertainty and change. No one can know exactly how the students in your school will learn how to eventually work together, and there will be many skeptics. Sometimes it's hard to change old habits, and there may be a few setbacks. Some areas will change immediately, while others will take a while to get going. Some people may feel no need to get involved. Some people will give all of their heart into opening up to other people or groups. Some people may be too shy or too afraid to make many changes at once. As individuals who make up the school system, some of us may have to change first to give others the courage to change too. Each of us in our own way has the potential to change the system for the better.

As more and more of us grow in our ability to be **Team Players, Straight Talkers** and **Peace Keepers,** the changes will become stronger. In the end, the old system will have transformed into a new kind of system because all of us, as individuals and in groups, directed our energy toward the goal of ending school violence. As we move toward the goal, we will see the results right before our eyes, hear the interaction, feel the friendship, and smell the security. When we take an active part in ending school violence, we take steps to change the lives of everyone in our school community. That's a big transition and a lot of commitment, and it's worth it!

Action:

1. How could you end or prevent violence in your school?
2. Are there any actions that you normally take that could change to better end violence in your school?
3. What action could you take today to start preventing school violence?

Life Winners:

Believe

Success and Empowerment

CORNERSTONE 4

Life Winners: Prepare for the Future

Life Winners Prepare for the Future and Take Action

Life Winners grab onto life's possibilities. They value each day, other people, and continuously learn. In other words, *Life Winners* enjoy what they do, explore what they want to learn, and share their learning enthusiastically with others.

Each *Life Winner* is unique. Every person alive is unique! Each of us has a combination of skills, beliefs, and experiences that no one else has. *Life Winners* have enough confidence in ourselves to try something new, even if it scares us a bit. We know that we must explore the world in order to figure out who we are, what we want to become, and how we can help others. Learning can mean meeting new people, exploring hobbies or careers, joining new groups, or making positive changes in ourselves. The more confidence we have to try new things, the more we can learn and grow.

"**Don't be afraid to fail. The road to success involves making mistakes as we try new ideas and explore new paths. Don't fear the future...embrace it!**"

To become a *Life Winner*, we first have to learn to be a *Team Player*—to work with others to help everyone win. The second part of being a *Life Winner* is communicating clearly, being a *Straight Talker*. The third element of winning in life is learning to calm people down, listen to their needs, and find win-win solutions—being a *Peace Keeper*.

These three skills lay the groundwork for our own success, because people love to work with others who help them win. *Life Winners* don't get stuck in ruts. We prepare for our future and take action. We help others succeed along with us. We all win.

As *Life Winners*, we can help end school violence for two reasons. First, we aren't afraid to explore new paths and new ideas for our own lives. Second, we value other people for who they are. We know that no one is perfect, but we also know that everyone has talents and skills that can complement our own. We can learn together with our teammates as we work toward our goals.

We can make contact with people who are experienced in some aspect of life. These guides, or mentors, can help us learn new ideas more quickly. Mentors can also gain our trust and become our friends. Who knows? A mentor might ask us to work with them or help us get a job. They have great connections with other experts, and they help us believe in ourselves. They encourage us to try new things and may become lifelong friends.

Using our own experiences, we can be mentors, too. In fact, we've probably already helped someone else learn. That's being a mentor. We just may not have thought about ourselves that way. People who encourage and help others are truly *Life Winners*. The big picture is one where we are all on the same team, connecting to create a community.

Action:

1. What is one thing that you can do everyday to prepare for your future?
2. How did you help someone else prepare for the future?
3. Have you ever been a mentor to someone?

Idea 38:

Stop Spinning Your Wheels!

When someone says they are, "spinning their wheels," it usually means that they are using time without moving forward in life. Sometimes we hear people say, "I'm stuck in a rut," or "I'm just getting by," when they describe their life. Maybe they got sidetracked somewhere, lost their motivation, or just did the minimum to get by. These expressions give us a good idea of the helplessness some people feel about the paths they've chosen. We each have the ability to move forward in life. We can focus on all things that are holding us back, all of the reasons why we could fail, and stay where we are. Or, we can focus on where we want to go with our lives, learn what it will take to get there, and start working towards our future. If we focus on the negative, we will not succeed. If we focus on the positive and start learning, we'll get there.

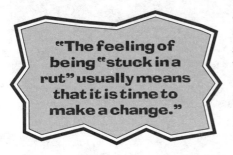

"The feeling of being "stuck in a rut" usually means that it is time to make a change."

A high school senior I once met in a leadership training program told me he didn't feel that he was going backwards in his life, but he felt that he had "plateaued." He was just doing the bare minimum to get by in school. He was passing all right, but he felt like he was headed nowhere. By doing the bare minimum, he was defeating himself from expanding his own potential for the future. What could he do? Some people feel "stuck in a rut" in a big way. They may be unhappy with something about their lives: a personal problem, school, family, a job that doesn't excite them. Being stuck can feel like being in the bottom of a deep hole with no way out.

I believe time is our most valuable asset, one that we can't replace once it's gone. We can't reverse time lost, but we can maximize the time we have. Take time to think through where you want to go. Decide if you are moving in that direction, staying still, or saying one thing and doing something else. Focusing your energy and time on achieving your goals will help you get there.

For instance, if you think you want to own a day care

center, run a gardening service, or train horses, go find out more about it. Share your dream and start learning. If you're unsure, talk with someone you trust and respect. Anything is possible if we believe in ourselves.

Action:

1. What are three positive things that you have accomplished in your life?
2. What are three goals that you'd like to reach in your life-time? Write them down.
3. What are you or could you be doing now to reach them?

I Have A Future!

To succeed in life, we have to believe we have a future. In working with youth, the scariest comment I hear is, "I have no future." When someone says this, I know that person feels as though he or she will not live much longer, that their life means nothing to them, or they feel they have nothing to contribute. This kind of thinking can do two things: make us unconcerned about the future, and not care if what we do results in something harmful to ourselves or someone else.

The most frightening part of people believing they have no future is that they don't care about what happens to them. If a person can't see their life lasting any longer than the next few months, it's hard for them to care about going to prison. Why should they care? They feel like they're not going to be around.

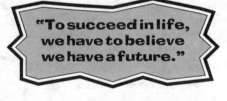

"To succeed in life, we have to believe we have a future."

Our society uses consequences—like prison—to stop people from committing crimes. Unfortunately, if a young person feels that they may not be here next week, then consequences don't work. People who can't see ahead to their futures can only focus on today.

A crucial step in ending school violence is helping students know that they have a future, that they will be here long-term, and that their life has real value. If you know someone who feels that their life won't amount to anything, take some time to let them know you care.

Notice what that person has to offer. **Everyone has** something to offer in the world. When you focus on what people **can do**, they begin to see themselves differently, too.

Action:

1. Do you feel that you have a future?
2. Do you know someone that feels that they have no future?
3. Have you ever told them that they **do** have a future?

Imagining Success Helps Us Succeed

We've all heard the saying, "Think positive." We may have ignored it like some old slogan, but there's a lot of truth in it. One of the best ways to help ourselves become successful is to imagine ourselves succeeding - in other words, to think positive. Imagining ourselves doing well moves us closer to our goals, boosts our confidence, and makes our work seem easier.

How other people see us is not nearly as important as how we see ourselves. If we don't see ourselves as successful we hurt our performance and fall short of our potential. Having negative thoughts about our abilities, criticizing our own actions, and mentally beating ourselves up actually makes us weaker. But when we imagine ourselves succeeding, we actually feel stronger and more capable. Maybe that means rehearsing mentally before we make a speech or practicing our best throw. It might mean planning how we might stop a confrontation, help a friend in need, or seeing ourselves as someone who can help end school violence.

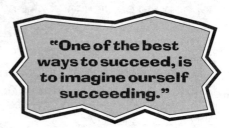

"One of the best ways to succeed, is to imagine ourself succeeding."

Many top athletes and performers spend part of their training time imagining themselves going through their entire event perfectly. Maybe they rehearse hitting the perfect shot over and over, making the almost impossible save, or delivering their best performance before a sold-out crowd. Mental practice supports physical training and enables athletes to do their best.

Mentally rehearsing will help us, too. Visualizing ourselves having an excellent performance does two important things. First, it helps us overcome fear. When we see ourselves failing in the future, we naturally become scared to act. Imagining ourselves succeeding gives us courage. Second, when we imagine ourselves doing things well, our minds and bodies make tiny little practice movements. These movements are so small we can barely feel them, but they are practice just the same.

And when we practice, we improve. Mental practice literally creates a map or guideline for action in our mind that we can follow. We must believe and imagine that we <u>can</u> end school violence, if we truly want to.

Action:

1. What is the most difficult challenge you will face in the next month?
2. Imagine succeeding and overcoming that challenge.
3. What could you do now to make that happen?

Idea 41 :

Losing:
When Life Puts Rocks in Our Path

At some point in our life, we may fail to reach a goal at which we've worked hard. For me it was not being accepted to my "ideal" college. I wanted to attend it for a long time. I worked as hard as I could to meet their requirements and sent my grades, scores and letters of application to the college on time. When I received their fancy white letter in the mail, I thought I was on my way. Instead, it was a rejection letter. At first, I was crushed. How could this happen? I worked so hard and then was not able to reach my goal.

Looking back, it was the best thing that ever happened to me, although I didn't know it at the time. The college that did accept me really was the perfect one for my needs. I made awesome friends and learned an incredible amount about life.

"The best way to overcome a setback is learn from it and keep moving forward."

Through that college I met my first formal mentor, who inspired me to make key decisions about my life. The new path I chose to take made me truly happy for the first time. It all started because I was rejected.

When we don't meet our goals or get what we want, we have to cope with loss, failure, or rejection or other problems. It's never fun and many times we feel really upset. Some people try to ignore the rejection. Others get angry. When they are angry, they can turn that anger on themselves, their friends, or the ones they feel rejected them. This setback or rejection is a "rock in our path," or a challenge that we will have to overcome.

The best thing I have learned to do when I don't reach the goal I want or when a challenge in life stops me in my tracks is to learn from it. I look at what happened, examine how I feel about it, figure out what I can do, then what I want to do. I try to see how my decision will affect me next month, next year or far into the future. Then I make my plans, refocus my efforts and move forward.

In life, we never truly lose as long as we continue learning and moving forward. We learn the most from our failures and can transform our losses into success if we choose. For instance, even if I hadn't been totally happy in that new college, it would have just meant that I had to keep on searching for the right path for me.

A key to ending school violence is dealing with setbacks and unforeseen challenges by learning from them and moving forward. We continue to succeed if we have the strength and belief to go on and plan out the route around the rocks in our path. We have not lost if we keep learning.

Action:

1. What setback have you faced lately?
2. How did you deal with it?
3. What was the end result?

Keeping A Journal, or Letters to Myself

On Jan 7, 1997 at 1:58 AM, my life went in a totally new direction based on a choice I made. I began writing in a journal and have continued every day since.

Now I know the reason why people keep journals. It isn't just to remember what we did in each day, but to let us "see" ourselves and "relive" a moment by writing it down. We spend so much of the day in motion—working, thinking, observing, interacting. Keeping a journal gives us time to remember and learn from our daily events as they happen. Writing is a way to listen to our feelings.

It can help us find answers to many of our own problems. Sometimes it's good to just unload what we are feeling, since keeping it inside only adds to our stress.

"How can I know what I think until I read what I write?"

It is important that our journals are private and that we are the ones who decide if anyone else reads them. That way, we can write down our most private thoughts and feelings. The key is to be honest.

There are many ways to write in a journal. Some people write a page a day every day. Others write a little, or only now and then. How much we write can depend on what's going on in our lives. A good reason to journal is to help us work out a big problem, one that stays on our minds. Writing a journal may not end our difficult times, but it can make them easier to deal with.

The days I learn the most from writing are when things maybe don't go the way I expected. Days like these can make me feel confused or frustrated, angry or sad. But my feelings and reactions always show me more about who I am. Sometimes I learn how to deal with certain people, new ideas, or concepts that challenge my beliefs. Other times, I find a new way to see the world around me and figure out how I fit into the bigger picture. It's interesting, too, because after a while, we can read back over how we felt or acted months or years earlier, and see how far we've come and what we learned. If more of us could release our feelings on paper rather than keeping them bottled up, we could help ourselves be more relaxed. Once we are more relaxed and understand ourselves better, we can help others to reduce the tension that leads to school violence.

Action:

1. Have you ever kept a journal?
2. What are three reasons why you should start a journal?
3. Try writing a journal entry about your day, today.

Idea 43:

Someone To Believe In Me:
The Power of Mentors

A mentor is a person we can trust, who gives us advice and supports us in some part of our lives. **Mentors are coaches who believe in us.** They are knowledgeable about life; they are also sources of experience, wisdom and encouragement in the areas of life we want to explore. Once we focus on an area of interest, finding a mentor in that area can make our path to discovery enjoyable. It's important for all of us to choose mentors who truly believe in and make time for us. We also have to put our time and energy into the relationship so the mentors know they're valued, too. That way we really benefit from each other's company.

A mentor may open the first door to discoveries in our area of interest. Since they are experienced in their areas, they often have friends who are willing to share their time or energy with us too. The more people we meet, the more doors will open. We may even decide to add another mentor!

"A mentor shares sincere belief in us...
..maybe more than we believe in ourselves."

Mentors encourage us to try new things; they are friends and lifelong contacts.

It's good to have more than one mentor, to add different perspectives. We can have mentors in all sorts of areas. For instance, some of us may be considering a career or facing a challenge. We might need a mentor for each. We may need a spiritual mentor for emotional support. We may admire the strength or friendliness of someone, and ask them to share their talent.

Mentors are from all walks of life. I was shy at first about getting a mentor; but I knew I needed help learning. More than anything else, I wanted someone I could trust, respect, and learn from, someone who absolutely believed in me. My mentors range in age from 28 to 74, are men and women, and have different backgrounds, races, and financial situations. My mentors have helped me through every challenge I've

132

encountered, embraced my failures and celebrated my successes.

One is a 42 year-old security guard who absolutely understands the challenges of growing up. Another is one of the richest people in America and a money-wise leader. Every one of them has helped me grow in some area of my life.

Mentors take negative feelings and turn them around for me. There were several times in my life when I can honestly say I do not know how I would have moved forward without my mentors. When I felt like I had a problem no one had ever been through, I found that at least one of them had the life experience I needed to know about. They all offered solutions. Suddenly it wasn't only me against any challenge. I had hundreds of mentor-years of combined experience to help me!

Of course, it is not enough to simply call a person you admire and say "Will you be my mentor?" They may not even know the word. First, you have to decide on the sort of help that you need. Then make a list of people who could help you. Your list can include people you know as well as those you don't. A mentor may be someone in your community, an adult you respect, or a famous athlete. When you contact them, tell them why you chose them—what knowledge and experience they have and why you need it. If they offer you time to talk, be on time for the meeting, and spend more time listening than speaking. Take notes on important ideas they have to offer. And don't forget to thank them for their effort: be sure to let them know how valuable they are to you.

Action:

1. What are three areas of your life that you want to improve?
2. What person or people do know who could help you with one or all three areas?
3. What would you say... how would you ask them to be your mentor?

You can learn more about mentors in my first book, ***Graduate To Your Perfect Job.***

Idea 44:

Choice:
The Spice Of Life

Everyday we face choices like what to wear or what to eat. Then there are the bigger choices like deciding what we want to do for the rest of our lives. I often hear adults say, "You will be making choices in the near future that will affect you for the rest of your life." Sure it's true, but *we make choices every day that affect us for the rest of our lives.* The added pressure of the future doesn't help us make better choices, it just adds stress or sometimes even fear.

When I have to make a really important choice, I always ask my mentors for advice. They've been around a lot longer and gone through more tough situations than I have. I may not always agree with their suggestions, but I always think about them—this gives me more options. It's really useful to me to get input from someone who has my best interests at heart; especially someone older. They always make me feel better about whatever choice I make.

There are several questions we can ask to help us make better choices: does this decision fit with my personal disciplines and long-term goals? If I shared my

"We make choices everyday that affect us for the rest of our lives."

decision with someone I truly care about, would they support it? Do my mentors or role models agree with my choice? Would I be embarrassed if people I cared about discovered my decision? Will I regret this choice later? Have I completely thought through all my options and alternatives?

Sometimes I like to write down all my options so I can see them more clearly. Good choices alone do not create success, but they do open doors. We should learn all we can about the choices we have, get advice from people we really value, and finally trust ourselves. Of all the people in the world, each one of us is the person who knows ourselves best. Don't do something because everyone else says it's what you *should* do. Wait for that gut feeling that lets you know what's right for you.

Action:

1. What is a big choice that you will make in the immediate future?
2. What are three things that are influencing your decision?
3. Talk with two people you respect about the big choice that you are facing.

Idea 45:

Share Yourself with Others:
Be A Friend and Mentor

All of us have heard, "It is better to give than to receive." This sort of sounds like "Give away your stuff." At this time in our lives, most of us don't have too many things, and what we do have we've saved for.

There is one thing we can give away that doesn't cost us money, though. That is our time. Giving our time, our effort and by genuinely caring about others will make more of an impression than any "stuff" we could give away. For example, a lot of times when we get a cool present from a friend, we're more touched by that friend's thoughtfulness and generosity than by the gift itself. Often that's because our friend has put so much thought and energy into getting it or giving it.

We can give by just being ourselves. How? By sharing our experiences and abilities, using our **Team Player**, **Straight Talker**, and **Peace Keeper** skills, and by opening our hearts to accepting others. Where can we do this? Any place that interests us where we can volunteer.

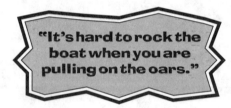

"It's hard to rock the boat when you are pulling on the oars."

A while back, I never thought I had the skills or opportunity to give. Then, a few years ago, I volunteered at a ranch designed for young people who were being given a second chance to move forward with their lives. These young people had trouble in their families or the towns they were from. At the ranch they had nice rooms, good food, a caring staff, excellent education and safe living at no cost. There were lots of other young people who could relate to them. All the ranch youth had to do was be responsible for their actions, help others, and be open to learning. So many young people working together for the good of everyone!

I knew the ranch was a special place. For two days I worked with teenagers my own age. My contribution was to be me—a non-violent person who works hard, believes he can be a life winner and finds value in everyone. In my own way, I helped them work on the mind set and skills they would need to succeed in the outside world.

Everyone there had a story. While we worked together, they talked about some of the problems in their lives that had held them back before, the violence they had to overcome in themselves and toward others, and the hope that the ranch had given them. Sometimes I talked and other times I listened, but I always believed in them. I return every year to help out.

Everyone can be a coach and a mentor in some way. We've all probably helped somebody—a friend, classmate, brother or sister—learn something. That's being a mentor. We just may not have thought about ourselves as mentors. People who help others learn about what they can do are truly life winners. We can all be mentors and volunteers.

One powerful way to mentor is to tutor someone else. Maybe they are a lot younger and you just read books with them. Perhaps you help someone learn math, or chemistry. Work with classmates on difficult assignments—mentor each other! Enroll in a community program designed to help other students. Sometimes adults need support. You can help them practice English, if it's not their first language. Older adults may need support and help around the house.

What's in it for us? Mentoring and tutoring can create friendships and connections that may last for years. Giving of ourselves lets us know that we're creating a more united and healthy community. It lets us explore more about our own interests. We can learn how strongly we feel about certain problems in the community by exploring our commitment to do something about them. To end school violence we all must give. **Nothing is more valuable than our time, and helping others is the greatest use of this precious resource.**

Action:

1. Who do you know that respects and admires you?
2. Do you think that you could help them in some way?
3. Let that person know that you are available, if they need help.

Tutoring Works A-Okay

Falling behind in school makes some of us frustrated, saddened, and can even put us on the path toward quitting school. I learned a valuable lesson early in high school: I always found a tutor or a friend who helped me learn tough subjects. At first, it seemed weird having a tutor, but I was falling behind in my work. I knew that if I got too far behind I would never catch up and was determined to not let that happen. It made all the difference in the world.

It seems that in high school there is group pressure to *not* have a tutor. The worst thing we can do is become too proud to ask for help, which can cause us to fall behind, get discouraged with education, and possibly dropout. But we do have a choice. We can admit we need help, work with a tutor and get better marks. Sometimes tutors are great just because they give us a different point of view or way of finding the solution. Learning disabilities can also be helped through a professional tutor. A common problem is dyslexia, or difficulty in learning to read: if you can't read it's hard to pass tests, no matter how smart you are. There are techniques that can fix this.

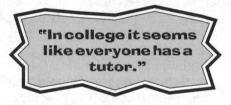

"In college it seems like everyone has a tutor."

Sure, you can fail a class or even drop out and always start again, but it may seem a lot harder the second time. The discouragement and image of falling behind may lead some of our friends to make excuses or self-defacing jokes about their performance. They may laugh as they tell us they made the lowest grade in the class. Some have excuses and reasons, like, "I just never tried," or "I had better things going on". Unfortunately, many of these friends can get left behind in a cycle of excuses and lack of achievement, because they don't have enough faith in themselves to get help from friends or professional tutors.

We have to change our point of view a little. Maybe the word "tutor" is the problem. Actually, *a tutor is a kind of mentor - a coach* for academic subjects. No one would put you down for working with a swimming coach or a basketball coach or a drama coach. Why should they with a math coach? Working with friends on assignments happens a lot with some people. In college it is OK to have a tutor. In fact, free tutoring is available in almost every subject.

No one has to get a 100 average or always earn the highest grades, you just have to do your best. Working with friends and other tutors or coaches helps us perform at our highest level, builds our confidence in our abilities, and keeps us moving forward. To end school violence we can help other students realize that they have the abilities to academically move forward with their life in order to achieve their dreams. It is not worth jeopardizing these dreams for some short-term action like self-violence through flunking out or school violence towards others.

Action:

1. Is there a class where tutoring would help you?
2. Who do you know that could help you with that class?
3. Ask them for help.

Idea 47:

Jumpstart to a Healthy Life

Sometimes we forget that **we are our bodies**, as much as we are our mind or our spirit. Our bodies are the way we sense that world: how we touch, taste and feel. Our bodies give us the means to explore and become better people. They're what we have in this life that allows us to grow emotionally and intellectually as well as physically. That's why it's so weird when some of us spend so much time on decorating the outside of our bodies, and don't take care of the rest of it.

Our bodies can give us so much more from life than just something to look like. Our strength, coordination, balance and speed depend on getting our minds and our muscles to work together. Our health is wrapped up in what we eat, how we exercise and what we feel about ourselves. Sometimes this has more impact on our health than even a major disease. Other

"By respecting our bodies we respect ourselves more."

people easily notice if we have a good physical and mental attitude. Staying healthy and getting in good physical condition gives us a force and dynamism that other people can see and feel. Being healthy also gives us energy: to work, study, pay attention, hike or sleep soundly.

Exercise also provides great stress relief and time to think through ideas and feelings. Eating healthy and sleeping well helps people make better decisions, have more energy and be better role models. By respecting our bodies we respect ourselves more, and have more ability and energy to handle issues with other people: a key to ending violence.

Sometimes we forget that unless we make an effort to maintain or improve our health now, we may not be as healthy in the near future. Taking care of our bodies is one of the best investments we can make at an early age, because it will affect us for the rest of our lives. We don't need to spend all our free time in a gym, either. Hiking, dancing, even mowing lawns will do it. The key is to consistently be active, eat better foods, and get a decent amount of sleep so we can be at our mental and physical best.

Action:

1. Do you think that you are healthy?
2. What are three things that you could do to be healthier?
3. Try them for one week.

Positively Powerful Reading

We are constantly bombarded with violent or depressing stories featured in television, the radio or the movies. Isn't there something positive happening in our world? Yes! Many books, Internet sites, and other resources focus on positive stories. These sources are important because inspirational, heartwarming or funny stories help us maintain our belief in the good in others and ourselves. These stories remind us about things in life that are both positive and necessary for our own emotional health. We need to know that people work for what they believe in and that small actions can make a huge difference. We need to know that all people are valued, and that we can overcome many barriers to help other people.

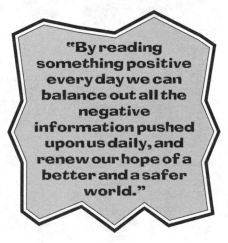

"By reading something positive every day we can balance out all the negative information pushed upon us daily, and renew our hope of a better and a safer world."

By reading something positive every day we can balance out all the negative information pushed upon us daily, and renew our hope of a better world and a safer world. In this way, we can get a well-rounded view of the world, and to our education. Of course, it's hard to be a hero all the time. But sometimes positive stories can provide us with the strength and support we need to carry out our own beliefs and positive actions in the world and build a strong foundation for our future.

Action:

1. Read something positive each day. I recommend the ***Chicken Soup for the Soul Series***
2. Write something positive each day.
3. Write something positive and give to a friend.

Saving Your Future by Saving For It

Managing money is a difficult thing, especially in high school. We never seem to have enough time for juggling school, extracurricular activities, work and money. Money! You can't live without it, but it's hard to live with what we have. Many young people get stressed about money; I know I did when I was in school. It seemed like I had to stretch every penny to the max to pay for all of my expenses. If I had planned just a little bit better, handling my finances would have been much easier.

We spend money in so many ways. There's plain hard cash, checks, credit cards, loans. Except for those dollar bills, each form of money has to be paid back, somehow. If we have checks, there's the monthly cost. If we have a credit card or a loan, there's interest. In other words, the people who let us have the money also add on a lot of profit for themselves. Sure, it's easy to think "I'll pay them back for those clothes in no time". But in the United States today, the average American adult owes over $15,000 in credit charges. At 10%, in yearly interest alone, that's $1,500! And you still owe $15,000! Credit cards charge up to 20%: that's $3,000 a year you could pay in interest!

"Planning what we're going to spend and save shows us we don't need much to get started. It lets us feel we are more in control of our own lives..."

So, the first rule for saving for your future is: **don't get into debt if you can help it**. Then you don't owe anybody their cash or their interest. The money that you save in interest alone is worth it. For example, some adults buy houses with a 30 year mortgage; that is they agree to pay back the loan, with interest, in 30 years. Do you know how much they end up paying by the time they're free and clear? Today, about **three times** the amount of the loan (so you buy a house for $50,000 but you actually pay $150,000!). Student loans for college may be necessary, but be careful: if you take out $10,000 in extra money to make it easy on yourself in college, you may be paying it back for 10 years to come. Borrow what you need, avoid giving into greed.

The second rule of saving for your future is: *figure out a budget you can work with and stick to it*. Some of us get an allowance. Some of us have a part-time job. Our parents may give us extra cash for clothes, school trips, or the weekend, but often they're working hard to get by just like we are. If we can keep to a budget we can work with the money we have and not go overboard. We can even begin to save.

The third rule to saving for your future is: *save and invest your money*. Let's look at it this way: small savings can add up week by week to a hefty amount if you just keep at it. Often we just don't do the math. Even if it's not in the bank where it can collect interest, $5 a week adds up to $260 in one year's time. By saving $10 a week for four years of high school, we'd graduate with $2080. With 5% annual interest you would have close to $2,400. That's not bad for $10 a week. The key is to keep it up and not take your savings out of the bank or out of an investment or bond. Us

"Your dollars will make dollars for you:
$
$ $
$$$$
$$$$$$$"

young people have time on our side. So it doesn't take much money invested NOW to be A LOT of money later. Allow your money to work for you. I recommend reading a basic investment book to gain a core understanding.

As youth, we have a huge advantage on our side - time. Time allows us to succeed if we also have the right information, advice, and some planning. It may be five dollars a week, it could be less or more, but saving in some way really adds up over time. We may not get rich quick, but wealth builds. The more money we earn the more we can invest if we don't spend it all. That's what budgets are for. Better budgeting also helps us avoid stressing over money and the future. Planning what we're going to spend and save shows us we don't need much to get started. It lets us feel more in control of our own lives, and that there is a way we can succeed without turning to violence.

Action:

1. How much could you save each week?
2. Where could you invest or save it?
3. Start this week and keep saving for one month.

Idea 50:

The Internet:
Downloading To End School Violence

We are the most technologically savvy generation ever. My seven year-old sister sends me constant e-mails, while my college-educated parents barely know how to turn on a computer. Some schools in America have no computers, while others have multi-million dollar technology labs. The Internet is a highway to great information, entertainment, and lots of not so good stuff.

The key to using the Internet is learning how to search for what you want and avoid all the junk and negative sites so frequently highlighted. I was intimidated using the Internet at first; it seemed like this huge web of places with no order or sequence; they were just out there waiting to be found. After getting help from a friend on using search engines and moving around on the Internet, I realized that it was simply a giant information resource. The Internet allows us to download all kinds of interesting things, listen to a live baseball game in another state, purchase anything imaginable, and communicate with people all over the world.

"We are the most techonology savvy generation ever. All the information can lead to good and bad thungs. A tool is only as useful as the people who use it."
www.endschoolviolence.com

We can multiply our efforts to end school violence by using the Internet as a tool to help end school violence. The Internet can allow youth from all over the country and the world to connect. We can share what works and what doesn't, communicate without travel, exchange useful information, and provide programs that help us accomplish our goals.

With this in mind we created **_www.endschoolviolence.com_** as an interactive destination for anyone who wants to get involved in ending school violence. The site will be safe for everyone and become a vehicle for people across the world to communicate, connect, and partner to end school violence. It will present the latest information from youth across America and other experts. An easy-to-use resource database will contain important information about youth violence prevention programs. For students the site will have scholarship applications for completing a service project that reduces violence. Bulletin boards will enable global sharing of ideas, and linked school homepages will display the progress of our programs. You can post your own ideas, observations, and activities on the site so other people around the world can learn from you. The idea is for visitors to communicate directly and build virtual discussion groups to reach beyond geographical barriers for innovative ideas and learning.

If you are under age 21, you can also join our youth organization, YouthConnect. It's totally free to become a member. This organization connects young people around the world to complete service projects to end school violence and build a larger sense of community. After visiting the site, please send us your input so we can continually add new features and learn. Using the latest technology, we gain an advantage in our movement to end school violence. We are the generation that can technologically come together.

Action:

      1. Visit ***www.endschoolviolence.com***
      2. Join **YouthConnect**
      3. E-mail your input and suggestions about the site.

In the End...

This can be the beginning of the end of school violence. Everyone who's read this book now knows the cornerstones and ideas and has probably worked though some or all of the action steps. I'd like everyone who reads this book to have been influenced in a positive way. I hope that all of us who have reflected and thought about the ideas the book contains will become more aware of:

- How individual and group communication can limit us or open doors,
- What our feelings are and what our bodies tell us,
- How others feel, what they say, and how they act,
- Differences in how we think when we're calm versus when we're upset,
- Ways we can be **Peace Keepers** with ourselves and others,
- The power each of us has to change our system and the world.

I love people. I believe in my heart that young people have the power to change their school communities and the world. One person deciding to act can begin an awesome transformation of an entire community system. In short, it takes you.

To make great changes from small actions, we have to take a stand. We have to stand by our beliefs and do what we say we'll do. We have to be the kind of person we'd like for a friend: someone we trust, who's fair, who's strong, who leads by serving.

It's important to act on our beliefs. I believe that violence is destructive. It can ruin friendships, families, property, and our sense of self worth. I believe that if enough of us connect to end violence, we can change society for the better.

Ending violence is about helping each of us better understand ourselves. It's about making each other aware of what kind of effect some of our "automatic" behaviors have on other people. It's changing our behavior to become more trusted, stronger, better-liked, and honestly valued as members of our communities.

The power of *connection* lies behind all these ideas on ending school violence. If we just can talk to each other—communicate—we can open the doors that keep us apart.

We can make more room for differences. We can talk to each other without being mean or fearful. When we talk as respected equals, we let others see who we really are, what we can do, and how we can work together. My vision is to share the tools we need to have the best and highest communication that we can.

When we change the way we relate to other people in our system, **we change the system**. Just by reading this book, even if we've made just one little change in ourselves, each of us has already changed the system. Think how much effect we'll have on school violence when we do more.

No matter who we are, it's impossible to work with people and not have occasional upsets. I'm still learning to recognize my own feelings, think positively and act in a healthy way when I'm angry, scared or frustrated. I've made a lot of changes in myself. I believe in myself and I know that every day I'll understand something new. If all of us start practicing to be *Team Players, Straight Talkers, Peace Keepers,* and *Life Winners*, we can all get better at managing our feelings. It's so important to manage the feelings that send us down potentially dangerous paths. My goal is to start with myself. I hope you share that goal.

I believe that by working together and using all of our creativity, we can end violence in ourselves and others. This is the reason I travel across America and talk with so many people. It's also the reason I started *YouthConnect.* We can help others to be the wonderful people they are inside, and we can support one another to succeed in life.

The great thing is, we can all succeed. We can grow and learn from each other all our lives because we are all different. The same skills that will help us end violence will also allow us to use and enjoy everyone's unique and special contributions. It takes communication to reveal everyone's potential. It will take action and determination from each of us to end school violence.

Please send me your feelings, your thoughts and your experiences. I value your input. I mean it.

Address: Jason Dorsey, President
World Institute to End School Violence
P.O. Box 49648
Austin, TX 78765

Visit our website, ***www.endschoolviolence.com***, and share them with us. Contribute your ideas to the entire learning system of youth in America.

Make it happen. Connect.

Action:

1. What is one thing you have learned from reading this book?
2. Please send me your input.
3. Give this book to a friend.

Resources...

Emotional Intelligence
by Daniel Goleman
Bantam Books, New York, 1995

System-Centered Therapy for Groups
by Yvonne Agazarian
Guilford Press, 1997

SPEAKING TOPICS

These programs and many others are available in both inspirational keynotes and in-depth seminars. For more information and availability, please contact Sondra Ulin at 512.259.6877 or via e-mail at: sondra@jasondorsey.com.

Jason Ryan Dorsey:

I. Peer Power: Speaking Youth to Youth

ENGAGE

Imagine the ability to reach youth of all backgrounds and aspirations on their level with proven wisdom, humor and experience. This is the power of twenty-one year old Jason Dorsey and his unique ability to connect with and engage youth. Jason's fresh perspective on the challenges and opportunities of youth bridges the disconnect to adulthood, builds self-esteem, and provides immediate actions for a meaningful future. Youth view Jason as a peer, he talks with them on their level, and they use what he shares.

BELIEVE

Encountering financial and family challenges from a young age, Jason was forced to adapt constantly. Believing in helping others, he began college at sixteen, attended five different colleges around the world, started a successful publishing company, and wrote a nationally acclaimed success book at age eighteen. Jason now devotes his life to helping others and focuses on youth.

His message of value and belief resonates with youth to create an openness for learning and embracing others.

INFLUENCE

Earning a Senior Partnership in The Everest Institute, a global human development organization, Jason accesses the most current information and strategies for enabling individuals to maximize their lives. Everest partners directly with governments, nations, and corporations to create widespread change that dramatically impacts the effectiveness of the organizations mission. Working with corporate executives, youth inmates serving life sentences, and everyone in between, Jason unleashes and reaches that hunger within each of us for living incredible lives.

**THE SKY IS NO LONGER THE LIMIT!

Breaking personal limitations, helping others through our actions, building self-esteem, networking,and committing to lifelong learning is critical to life success. Jason Dorsey shares these mindsets and much more in his interactive, hilarious, and power-filled programs.

- Connects with students of all backgrounds and mindsets
- Builds trust and belief with students
- Walks his talk of taking control of ones life
- Establishes personal expectations, long-term thinking
- Helps them take responsibility for their actions
- Customized to reach event goal with Jason's zest for life

These programs and many others are available in both inspirational keynotes and in-depth seminars. For more information and availability, please contact Sondra Ulin at 512.259.6877 or via e-mail at: sondra@jasondorsey.com.

Jason Ryan Dorsey:

II. Sharing a Fresh Perspective For Educators

ENGAGE

Entering a large room filled with educators of all backgrounds and experiences, Jason's youth and incredible energy draw attention and curiosity. Within minutes Jason connects with the audience, extinguishes their skepticism, and engages them on their level. Barely twenty-one years old, Jason works with educators throughout the US to help them better connect, motivate, and influence youth. He ignites their original passion for improving young lives and shares the value and impact they deliver daily.

INSPIRE

Encountering financial and family challenges from a young age, Jason was forced to adapt constantly. Teachers immediately moved to the forefront of his life and influenced much more than his education. They encouraged him to keep moving forward and devote his life to learning. Believing in helping others, he began college at sixteen, attended five different colleges around the world, started a successful publishing company, and wrote a nationally-acclaimed book at age eighteen. Now only 21, Jason devotes his life to helping the group that changed his life and millions more each year: EDUCATORS. Bridging the dynamic responsibilities of educators and the needs of youth, Jason provides powerful strategies and actions for long-term results. Working with over 150,000 people annually, Jason skillfully turns any skepticism about his age into an openness for learning and embracing new ideas.

INFLUENCE

Earning a Senior Partnership in The Everest Institute, a global human development organization, Jason accesses the most current information and strategies for enabling individuals to maximize their lives. Everest partners directly with governments, nations, and corporations to create widespread change that dramatically impacts the effectiveness of the organization's mission. Working with corporate executives, youth inmates serving life sentences, and everyone in between, Jason unleashes and reaches that hunger within each of us for living incredible lives. Educators engage his youthfulness, praise his insight, laugh and cry with his stories, and implement his message.

**ACHIEVING GREATNESS FOR ALL YOUTH!

Bridging modern youth with the changing responsibilities of educators, Jason knows firsthand what it takes to reach, inspire, and teach youth. Jason's powerful personal story of how educators changed his life grabs them on a professional and personal level. Jason's passion for education, excitement for life, and humor-filled approach transform his message into immediately applicable actions for enhancing our living and education experience.

- Builds trust quickly with educators
- Teaches communication strategies that engage ALL youth
- Shares belief and value for educators and their growing responsibilities
- Enables educators to overcome obstacles in areas outside their profession
- Re-ignites the passion educators have for learning and building futures
- This program and many others are available in both inspirational keynotes and in-depth seminars.

Jason's Motivation:

Twenty-one-year-old Jason Dorsey is a young person who has chosen to make a difference in the lives of others. While growing up in a single-parent family in a small community in Central Texas, Jason quickly learned to shape his own future by making wise choices. At age 18, after attending courses at 5 colleges, Jason was preparing to graduate from the University of Texas with a 4.0 GPA when he heard a guest speaker that changed his life. That speaker, now a mentor to Jason, challenged him to do more with his life.

Jason noticed a desire for direction, a lack of motivation and a scary feeling of hopelessness in the lives of the youth around him. To fill this void, Jason wrote **Graduate to Your Perfect Job**. This reader-friendly book shows young people exactly how to begin taking command of their future. Jason's simple 6-step process is a comprehensive guide for obtaining the career of their dreams. Then, to speed up the publishing process so teenagers could have immediate access to the book, he founded an educational publishing company.

Jason's Mission:

With the success of the book, Jason began speaking professionally to youth of all different backgrounds across the country. During the past 3 years, Jason has become the most sought after young speaker in America. As he visited with today's youth, he vividly discovered that school violence is the issue foremost in their minds. Jason knew he had to share his positive solutions and unique perspective from working with over 150,000 youth and the **World Institute to End School Violence** (WIESV) was created.

Jason has now combined the candid insight and solutions from thousands of young people, along with in-depth input from leading educators and parents, in **Can Students End School Violence? Solutions from America's Youth**. This action-oriented book gives real solutions to end violence in our schools. The focus is on what each of us can do in our own lives and communities to stop this life-shattering trend. Jason listens to youth and is committed to sharing their perspective.

Jason's Message:

Jason and his team are working diligently to share his message and the message of youth across America. Jason's message is one of hope and a positive call to action for you and your community. With your help, we will create a safe future for our young people.

For more information and availability, please contact
Sandra Ulin 512-259-6877
or via e-mail at sondra@jasondorsey.com.
Visit our website at www.jasondorsey.com.

KEY INITITIATIVES FROM
THE WORLD INSTITUTE TO END SCHOOL VIOLENCE
(WIESV)

1. AWARENESS: Spreading the word that immediate solutions direct from youth are available.

A. We will launch a public relations campaign sharing ideas from youth about actions we can all take to reduce school violence.

B. _**www.endschoolviolence.com**_ will be the Internet destination for information, communication, and solutions to ending school violence.

C.Donating copies of **Can Students End School Violence?** to educators, students, parents, and community leaders.

2. IMPLEMENTATION: Turning our solutions from youth into actions.

A. Our soon-to-be-released supplementary curriculum will take the concepts from this book and transform them into a program for middle schools and high schools.

B. Grow our student organization, YouthConnect, to bring together students from across America to take actions towards ending school violence.

C. Train educators across America on methods, strategies, and actions to shape the social climate at their school, better connect with youth, and end school violence.

3. MEASUREMENT: Tracking the results of our programs.

A. Through our social climate evaluation tool we will be able to measure the change in the social climate of a school through the implementation of our program.

B. We will also be able to track the number of new student mentors, students gaining adult mentors, new student volunteers, and hours volunteered.

C. Customize our programs to meet the specific needs of the school implementing the supplementary course.

World Institute to End School Violence
CORNERSTONE QUESTIONS

To What End?

The World Institute To End School Violence is a nationwide student-lead movement to end violence in schools. We focus on youth and their perspective to deal directly with ideas, behaviors, and actions that lead to school violence. Tragic episodes of school violence, as discussed throughout America, are at the extreme end of the violence continuum and statistically declining. But smaller actions, those that can build into tragic episodes of school violence, are epidemic. The young people of America shared their input with us and we are responding. We will bring together entire communities of youth across America to work together to end the epidemic of actions and interactions that can lead to tragic episodes of school violence.

How do we define School Violence?

School violence is any action that negatively impacts the social climate within a school. Our focus is on school violence that directly comes from and affects youth.

Why do most Children become Violent?

Most children who become violent towards themselves or others feel rejected and psychologically victimized.
Early Warning: Timely Response-A Guide to Safe Schools

What does this have to do with School Violence?

Any school social climate that fosters unequal relationships within its student body and rejects certain members within that student body as not good enough, not smart enough, not pretty enough, not rich enough, etc. at the same time fosters school violence. Being a teenager is all about figuring out who we are in a time of major life change, and one of the ways we begin to create an identity is to join groups often with people like ourselves or like how we want to be seen. This division of students leaves some feeling superior and others rejected. As students become more rejected they can get angry and turn that anger towards themselves, the people who rejected them, or the greater school community, this can build into school violence.

What Youth Told Us

After working with over 150,000 youth across America, 20 year-old Jason Dorsey learned firsthand that mentoring students to create strong relationships with their peers, regardless of social group, is absolutely essential to ending school violence. An early warning sign of weakness within a school community are students being isolated and victimized. Students do not need to always agree or wear the same clothes, but they all need build strong connections with other students and value each other.

School Violence is not only Guns

School violence is not only guns and fists. School violence is the eighth grade boy that sits in the back of his English class and is afraid to ask questions because other students might laugh at him. School violence is the sixth grade girl that eats alone every day because somehow the other students feel she is different from them. School violence is the captain of the football team that knows everyone but feels there is not a friend his age he can trust. School violence is the shy child who walks down the halls each day, does not get a single 'hello', and is numb to relationships because he has had his trust broken so many times. School violence is the high school senior who finally believes the people who repeatedly told him 'he has no future' and then violently complies with their judgement.

What does the term Social Climate mean?

Social climate is about four key relationships: the relationship of a student to themselves, a student to their peers, a student to their parents, and a student to their educators. Shaping these four relationships through our violence prevention movement, we can shape an entire school community.

How does School Violence Start?

School violence often starts subtly, quietly, almost unnoticeably. Small things lead to school violence. It can begin at home with a lack of strong connections between a student and their parents, making it difficult to build new relationships. It can grow as a student enters school and feels inferior academically. It builds as a student is rejected and victimized and lacks the essential connections needed to end school violence. The cycle can stop abruptly with one great teacher, one great friend, one great parent, one great community member, one great student movement.

Can Students actually End School Violence?

Yes! Ultimately, they are the only ones who can. If we do not shape schools from the inside (students first), we have not altered the people that create and are affected by school violence. Metal detectors, video cameras, and other devices meant to make schools safer, do not necessarily bring students together or make them feel increased value. To end school violence we must start with the students' perspective and build the strong connections throughout their social climate they need to build a safe and connected school community.

| CAN STUDENTS END SCHOOL VIOLENCE? Solutions from America's Youth | GRADUATE TO YOUR PERFECT JOB |

☐ I want to order **Can Students End School Violence?** *Solutions from America's Youth*
Please send me _____ copies X $14.95 (plus $2.50/book S&H)
for the enclosed amount of $ _____

☐ I want to order **Graduate to Your Perfect Job!**
Please send me _____ copies X $14.95 (plus $2.50/book S&H)
for the enclosed amount of $ _____

☐ I want to order **GTYPJ-INTEGRATED TEACHER'S CURRICULUM**
Please send me _____ copies X $35.00 (plus $2.50/book S&H)
for the enclosed amount of $ _____

QUANTITY DISCOUNTS AVAILABLE TO EDUCATORS
For details, please contact:
Golden Ladder Productions
(512) 259-6877
or
visit Jason's website at www.jasondorsey.com

Method of payment

_____ Cash _____ Check _____ Money Order _____ Purchase Order
(Payable to Golden Ladder Productions.)

Name _____

Address _____

City _____ State _____ Zip _____

Phone _____ E-mail _____

Return to:
Golden Ladder Productions
P.O. Box 49648
Austin, TX 78765
www.jasondorsey.com

CAN STUDENTS END SCHOOL VIOLENCE?
Solutions from America's Youth

GRADUATE TO YOUR PERFECT JOB

☐ I want to order *Can Students End School Violence? Solutions from America's Youth*
Please send me _____ copies X $14.95 (plus $2.50/book S&H)

for the enclosed amount of $ _____

☐ I want to order *Graduate to Your Perfect Job!*
Please send me _____ copies X $14.95 (plus $2.50/book S&H)

for the enclosed amount of $ _____

☐ I want to order *GTYPJ-INTEGRATED TEACHER'S CURRICULUM*
Please send me _____ copies X $35.00 (plus $2.50/book S&H)

for the enclosed amount of $ _____

QUANTITY DISCOUNTS AVAILABLE TO EDUCATORS
For details, please contact:
Golden Ladder Productions
(512) 259-6877
or
visit Jason's website at www.jasondorsey.com

Method of payment

_____ Cash _____ Check _____ Money Order _____ Purchase Order
(Payable to Golden Ladder Productions.)

Name _____

Address _____

City _____ State _____ Zip _____

Phone _____ E-mail _____

Return to:
Golden Ladder Productions
P.O. Box 49648
Austin, TX 78765
www.jasondorsey.com

BOOKS & INTEGRATED TEACHER'S CURRICULUM
ORDER FORM

CAN STUDENTS END SCHOOL VIOLENCE? Solutions from America's Youth	**GRADUATE TO YOUR PERFECT JOB**

☐ I want to order *Can Students End School Violence? Solutions from America's Youth*
Please send me ____ copies X $14.95 (plus $2.50/book S&H)
for the enclosed amount of $ _____

☐ I want to order *Graduate to Your Perfect Job!*
Please send me ____ copies X $14.95 (plus $2.50/book S&H)
for the enclosed amount of $ _____

☐ I want to order *GTYPJ-INTEGRATED TEACHER'S CURRICULUM*
Please send me ____ copies X $35.00 (plus $2.50/book S&H)
for the enclosed amount of $ _____

QUANTITY DISCOUNTS AVAILABLE TO EDUCATORS
For details, please contact:
Golden Ladder Productions
(512) 259-6877
or
visit Jason's website at www.jasondorsey.com

Method of payment

____Cash ____Check ____ Money Order ____ Purchase Order
(Payable to Golden Ladder Productions.)

Name _____
Address _____
City _____ State _____ Zip _____
Phone _____ E-mail _____

Return to:
Golden Ladder Productions
P.O. Box 49648
Austin, TX 78765
www.jasondorsey.com